"*The whole work edifies in its cele*
between nature's awesome power ɑ
their limits."

US REVIEW OF BOOKS (2021) BY MARI CARLSON.

**FIFTH
EDITION**
Revised and
Expanded

ALAN V. GOLDMAN

REFLECTIONS
ON
Mountaineering

A JOURNEY THROUGH LIFE
as Experienced in the Mountains

BOOKSIDE Press

ISBN: 978-1-77883-055-6 (Paperback)

   978-1-77883-056-3 (Hardback)

   978-1-77883-057-0 (Ebook)

BookSide Press
877-741-8091
www.booksidepress.com
orders@booksidepress.com

Dedication

I dedicate this book to all future climbers and would-be climbers who would sally forth in search of their magic Mountain. The rewards are intangible and evanescent, the risk is real, but the goal is one of ineffable joy, indeed, ecstasy, in both the process of climbing itself and in the attainment of its purposes. And remember this: there's a mysterious glory and nobility to be found in the *im*perfect, so long as the goal is worthy. As the poet Robert Browning wrote: *"Ah, but a man's reach should exceed his grasp, Or what's a heaven for?"* "Andrea del Sarto," lines 97-98 (emphasis added).

Read About What's At The Top And What Comes Before

Retired lawyer Alan V. Goldman spent a substantial amount of his personal time climbing the high mountains. As a mountaineer, he's gained various insights into human nature, the nature of reality, and, indeed, the meaning of life itself. At the age of sixty-three, a revelation came over him: it was time to reveal the many truths he's come to realize. The result has been a unique account of a person's journey into sublime light and utter darkness.

In the Book, poetry meets adventure. Presented as one hundred thirty-eight narrative-style poems, some of which rhyme and others are in blank verse, ***Reflections on Mountaineering:*** *A Journey Through Life as Experienced in the Mountains (Fifth Edition, Revised and Expanded: 2023)* summarizes much of what the author learned in his more than thirty years of climbing. This variety of style is altogether appropriate because a mountaineer experiences the secret facets of his obscure desire both in poetic terms and in "blank verse"—all offering a fleeting glimpse into the hidden aspects of a mountaineer's experiences. Readers can take away what Goldman has learned about the phenomenon of "Flow"—athletes would recognize this as being in the "Zone," which is thought to exist when people are content because their capabilities are adequate to meet their responsibilities. See ***Mountain Experience***: *The Psychology and Sociology of Adventure,* by Richard G. Mitchell, Jr. (The U. of Chicago Press: 1983) at pp. 153, 177, *passim.* Indeed, the very purpose of achieving such a state of being is to facilitate the ability to create human meaning out of nothingness — where "nature has left nothing other than a blank on the map". Further, various philosophical—type musings on what can be called existentialist principles are partly an outgrowth, in the intersection of mountaineering and meditative poetry, of the universally recognized seminal work, **Being and Nothingness** (***L'Être et le néant***)(1943), by the widely influential thinker Jean-Paul Sartre.

Ultimately, the Book recognizes that the "Quest" that drives climbers strongly relates to the notion expressed in the Declaration of Independence about the "unalienable right" of mankind to the "Pursuit of Happiness" — a right for which governments are instituted among men to protect.

Further, Goldman maintains that many of the same moral issues that confront us in everyday life are present in the high mountains, only to a sharper degree. Musing on topics such as awe and wonder, fear and how to confront it, the lure of the big mountains, as well as the role of luck, fate, and chance, Mr. Goldman makes accessible to the general public the otherwise "hidden" truths that mountaineers regularly experience. Further, many of the poems address the human perception of reality in the context of the meaning of life itself, and of how climbers impart meaning to the mountains by the very act of climbing them. Of course the poems deal with the feelings evoked by striving for success in the mountains, but also cope with the trauma of defeat. Above all, there is meaning to be found in the very preparation and discipline required for the act of mountaineering, as well as in experiencing the elation of conquest — of both the mountains and ourselves.

Moreover, Goldman says that the moral "lesson" readers could mine from the Book is that serious mountaineering is not just a trivial, risk-adventure sport played by adrenaline junkies: No, "it is a bold endeavor requiring the most determined and committed individuals who have a sense of history and a respect for the context in which they follow their ambition" as Goldman explains.

In sum, the book is a refreshingly effective comparison of ordinary life with mountaineering. The poems are meant to speak to mature, generally well-educated adults who have not had much, if any, experience of life in a mountain environment, and to make that life readily accessible and comprehensible to that audience.

Written with this expansive audience in mind, readers (mountaineers or not) surely will find something of value with which to relate, such as the striving for success and the fear of defeat. This Book is certainly a worthwhile read for anyone on a perpetual pursuit to attain new heights and insights.

Mr. Goldman is a graduate of Horace Mann School, 1975; Harvard College, 1979; and Harvard Law School, 1982. In addition to his mountaineering adventures as his avid avocation, he practiced law for many years and is now retired.

Introduction

Please visit the author's website at mountainreflections.art

These poems seek to convey the essence of my experiences in the high mountains, or those of my friends and fellow climbers. They also contain my insights into the inner meanings present in those climbs, as well as my musings on the "meaning" of life itself.

It is my hope that you will reach your own perceptions of the significance of my adventures, and explore your own feelings about the significance of the actions of those who strive to attain what seems the impossible in an environment hostile to their living, much less thriving.

Moreover, even despite the air of certainty that the most accomplished and skilled climbers would like to project about their goals and achievements, We believe, as is revealed in the Scripture *of Ecclesiastes*, 9:11-12, that the vagaries of time and chance still govern their circumstances, which are always liable to being overtaken by unexpected misfortune.

For, as the Scripture further relates, no one can know when their time has come; and like fish entangled in a fatal net, or like birds taken in a snare, so, too, are the most competent and wise of humans like prey who are trapped when a time of catastrophe falls suddenly upon them. *See Eccl. supra*, personal translation; (compare the translations in various versions: KJV, NKJV, NRSV, NIV, and JPS).

From these dark truths, I believe that climbers struggle to impress human meaningfulness upon a blank slate that would otherwise remain but a void.

This existential struggle to create meaning out of nothingness provides the impetus that drives climbers on to perform feats that defy nature, and seek to infuse that nature with meaning, wherever it has settled on a verdict of vacancy and emptiness. This indeed is the climber's clarion call: to fulfill the work of Creation where nature itself has left only a blank on the map.

It is my earnest hope that my poems will shed light on this hidden corner of Creation that lacks for nothing but the will to find human meaning where, before, there had been none at all.

Table of Contents

Bonus Materials

Preface
to Third Edition

To my readers:

Please note that there are *thirty-six* new poems (in comparison to the first edition of this Book) present in this *Third Edition.*

The first twenty poems below are placed under previously existing subheadings, while poems 21-30, below, are all placed under an entirely new subheading entitled: "**Private Thoughts**". Likewise, poems 31-36, below, are all placed under an entirely new subheading entitled: "**Bonus Materials**" In sum, the thirty-six new poems are entitled:

1. *Moonlit Mountain*, on p. 32
2. *Idealized Perfection*, on p. 36
3. *Snowbound Giant: Object of My Desire*, on p. 37
4. *Solitary Motion in the Wake of an Avalanche*, on p. 40
5. *Aftermath of an Avalanche*, on p. 41
6. *Bailing out on Twining Peak*, on p. 58
7. *Anxious Doubt*, on p. 61
8. *Frustration at the Foot of Forbidden Peak*, on p. 74
9. *Fearsome Peak: North Face*, on p. 75
10. *Lost Pinnacle*, on p. 77
11. *Nature's Handiwork*, on p. 92
12. *Character of the Ideal Rope Partner*, on p. 96
13. *Scene of the Avalanche*, on p. 104
14. *The Test*, on p. 106

Also, please notice that the poem *Coda,* which previously appeared on p. 95 of the First Edition, now appears on p. 126.

Preface

Preface to the Fourth Edition (Revised and Expanded: 2022)

Please note that (in addition to a number of minor editing revisions) *there are five new poems in this Fourth Edition (Revised and Expanded: 2022):*

Trapped (at p. **42**);

Disaster Viewed from Afar and Near (at p. **62**);

Glorious Failure? (at p. **120**);

Despondency Challenged (at p. **214**); and,

My Finale (at p. **225**).

Preface

Preface to FIFTH Edition (2023)

To my readers;

Please note that this new FIFTH Edition has an entirely new Section containing eighteen new poems, entitled: *"Afterthoughts,"* which is found beginning at *p. 230* of the FIFTH Edition.

Preface

Preface to FIFTH Edition (Revised and Expanded: 2023)

To my readers;

Please note that (in addition to some minor editing revisions) there are seven new poems in this *Fifth Edition (Revised and Expanded: 2023)*, all of which have been added to the Section entitled *"Afterthoughts,"* beginning at *p. 246*, namely:

49. ***On the Brink of a New Life?*** (at p. **246**);

50. ***Falling Drops*** (at p. **248**);

51. ***Keeping up the Pace*** (at p. **249**);

52. ***Peculiar Progression Toward the Far Distant Unknown*** (at p. **250**);

53. ***Rumination upon Reaching the Summit*** (at p. **251**);

54. ***Delicacy Amidst Terror*** (at p. **252**); and,

55. ***Expression of the Will*** (at p. **253**).

Reality and Dreams

Being and Nothingness

"Barren, yet brazen, bold and beautiful for you to behold —
My summit glistens with morning dew — etched into hoarfrost
  Cloaking my native peak, and still more with your passing like a mirage,
My summit shimmers with an unearthly refraction,
trembling from
Your evanescent embrace, reflecting your stamp of individuality to
create the ultimate
Existential act of impressing meaning out of nothingness."

See the mountain's clouds of clearing haze, as though the mountain is saying:
"Here am I: see how easy it would be to crawl up my highest flanks, to scale me in a day!"
Just then, like a woman having temptingly hiked up her skirt, only so far and no further,
The mountain's pall descends and shrouds it in a whirl of snow, clouds, and ice, covering its summit
With the mist of my dreams, as if flirting with me.

The vision of wonder is thus withdrawn in a moment of absence and gloom shading my peak.
"See here," the mountain might say: *"I was but the quintessence of nothingness until you forced your will upon my*
Blank form, and by your striving imparted meaningfulness to my abidingly neutral presence,

Signifying the ultimate mark of the reality of humanity's trek upon a void of vacancy,

Futility, and suffering; only by then will you have imparted to me the meaning of your sojourn my way —

And I know that I am fated to stand solitary again after your travails are completed."

Mountain of My Dreams

Ah, mountain of my dreams, you are shaped like a diamond crystal,
Sharp ridges and flat faces combining into one harmonious whole;
Where is your flaw, your most vulnerable point, line, or crack?
If put to the test, would you spin in eternity or topple of your own weight?
For nature knows of no perfection, only maps of half-realized proportions
that we must complete in our own mind's eye: pure, symmetrical, and
rigorously intact.

Ah, mountain of my dreams, will you spur me on to achieve the impossible and
Travel where the very presence of humans was not foreseen?
Will you enable me to walk into a picture postcard, or will you deflate my
aspiration of
Ever attaining the pristine, quintessential model of this broken world?

Would Plato be distraught if we equated the mundane and the spiritual plane
to find that there
Is still glory in the imperfect, in the striving after a receding horizon that is
unknown in
The realm of the ideal?

Ah, mountain of my dreams, nothing do we perceive that is not imperfect,
Only uncompleted thoughts, ideas, and visions of the wholly coherent world
yet to come,
While we await your magical presence in our midst.

Mountain Ballad

Just a ridgeline far away,
Just a trek there in three days
So when I see the plains erupt
With angry, jagged peaks:
My heart stops pounding for I'm serene
That all is perfect in this scene.
Protected by a moat of gullies,
No one ventures to sally the route
Waiting to greet us bullies
Who dare to storm your mountain's fastness without guilt.
Going along the winding trail,
I spy a cub bear on a rock alone;
But this must mean you're within your mother's smell and hail,
Which can't be far afield of that mountain stone where you do roam.
Talking loudly to my partner
Is standard procedure to give warning fair
For bears do retreat at the sound of us
But your mother's duty is to know
That our trail be not close to you.
We pass between the mother and cub
Raising our voices as though in alarm
For you do flee the humankind.
Yet none of you emerge to see
That we have long since passed and left the cub to be.
If we meet an angry mother,
We must yield, for this park is her preserve

In a state of nature, where human life is scarcely tolerated.
We finally reach around the bend
When emerges the knife-edged ridge
Covered with a thin, translucent *verglas* coat of ice,
Which amply explains our fear of your ledges.
That small quiver in our gut of naked fright
Stands us speechless as we prepare our ropes, slings, carabiners, cams, and crampons
And many other things lashed tight and right.
For surely we don't seek to entangle or miss the mark.
Slowly we cross the glacier's bottom, where a shadowy dimple in the snow may send us deep under.
Gaining purchase on the rocky ridges and ledges, we sigh with relief,
Still not knowing what to expect from your spinning winds
and slippery sides.
So one foot after another and another til we top your cap in sheer wonder.

I brought to the mountain many worries
And it returned them in a brilliant display
Of icy majesty and harrowing features that
Did return me to my boyhood dreams without delay.

Pentimento

Glancing upward I behold
A perfect realm of apex stronghold —
But this world knows of no such perfect place
So you must claim some kindred space.

Behold the goings-on below
Enticing the hordes of Seekers
To scramble through your endless maze
Of refuge and redoubt—far from city grime and haze.

I return to your reflection for renewed strength
Whenever I feel my body's growing feeble.
Solely by your challenge above, I can *see* the way before me while I rest;
Or else, no simple matter, I must endure pure *ennui.*

Where does one controlled by your pythonic mass of rubble
Go to make me fail to stumble? I thus hesitate,
Repentant of my headstrong plan to penetrate your maze that makes
Me so apt to flounder and fumble.

What Is a Mountain's Meaning for Mankind?

What is a mountain but a feature of the grimy profane?
What is humanity but a spark of the purest sacred divine?
As Blake said, "Great things are done when men and mountains meet";
A merging of our forms until the world is more complete?
Do we humanize the mountain by investing it in ourselves?
Or does the mountain subsume us into its mundane shell?

As Muir once said: "We are now in the mountains and they in us";
Do they challenge us to struggle just to stand upon their tops?
Or are we in the grip of some *idee fixe*?
No—we challenge and conquer "nothing but ourselves" as Mallory once
humbly said.
The mountain stands as a testament that not all things were made
With any thought of mankind, but still serve as a vehicle for us to demonstrate
great feats.

Immutable, truly timeless in the lives of mortals
The mountain remains passive, and yet is so attractive;
The mountain has the power of virtual
gravity drawing us into its mass;
This power of attraction was certainly not conceived by us
Nor is it useful to our being, but is subtle and sublime;
For to climb upon a mountain's flanks is but an active form of meditation
that earns us nothing to our material gain,
Yet adds immeasurably to the memories in our brains.

The mountain is inanimate, but we have vitality and the freedom to choose our path,

Hither and yonder, while the mountain remains fixed in its place.

Is it not we who gyrate and survey 'round the mountain's
various faces and ridges
To ascertain "the most practicable," "the most beautiful,"
and "the most difficult" route
To the summit—and are not these concepts solely human, lodged in our
solipsistic vision
Of the world in which we think ourselves, freedom to choose notwithstanding,
to be virtually in a prison?

On Reality and Dreams

How happy I am to be free of abstract worries;
Your mass focuses my attention onto palpable realities
Where the only thing that counts is the next step I take,
Because I'm bound up in your micro-reality of reactive causality.

Immediately, I apprehend the consequence of my error;
Sharp rebuke is your standard modality of expression:
Rope too short, sloppy knot, untied laces—each claims its partner
In its fatal embraces. Not planning ahead for particular places
Takes its toll by marking my future boundaries.

Most certainly, my not planning ahead for particular events
Limits my future horizons beyond which—at the very least—
I'll never reach since I didn't foresee your problematic pitches.

Unlike in boys' games, there are no "do-overs" nor reset buttons;
The thing when it happens is indelibly etched
Into the sequence of events that ineluctably ensues without relent.

The mountain is passive, but inspires creative action;
It won't be made malleable; instead, is rigid and fixed
Except when it avalanches and engulfs everything before it.

Above all, the mountain remains stolid, indifferent, uncaring, unfeeling.
This fixed truth is neither cruel nor wanton;
It just *is*, like the force of gravity affects all alike;
Indeed, like the mountain itself just "is," simply, as Mallory said, "because it's there".

Yet something more lurks in your scarred gullies and scree;
Something wondrous, something evanescent, as if in a dream.

What Is a Mountain That We Should Take Notice?

What is a Mountain but an eruption of earth
Devoid of significance except what we impart to it
By our efforts to achieve feats of great wonder:
We invest in the Mountain the lore of the climbers' travails.

Look at the North Face of the Eiger, also known as the White Spider, for all
the would-be
Conquerors it is comprised of interlocking features with all having names
with meaning
Infused into the Mountain by cadres of prior devoted Seekers who imposed
their
Meanings, their very own being onto its blank form—
An existential act of human dimension
Pressed onto the formations of the Mountain. The litany, by ascending
sequence, being: the First Pillar, the Shattered Pillar, the Gallery Windows,
the Difficult Crack, the
Hinterstoisser Traverse, the Swallows' Nest, the Ice Hose, and then the First
Ice Field,
the Second Ice Field, the Third Ice Field, the Flat Iron, Death Bivouac, the
Ramp, the Traverse of the Gods, the White Spider, and only then the Exit
Cracks, the Summit Ice Field, and, finally, should
You still be alive, the Summit at 13,024 feet.

To create directed meaning through one's own *choices* that supplant amorphous conditions is the very hallmark of existential action, where

Each name represents a locus of Mountain lore created by climbers who had gone before, and struggled and either triumphed or failed to achieve the object of their obscure desire.

To those who would follow the route pioneered by so many others, a route that still

Offers no assurance of success, takes a braver human than one who departs from the

Line established by generations of climbers. A mechanical aid *direttissima* approach

Has been successfully negotiated, but is not practical for most others seeking to climb

This Mountain by exploiting the natural flaws in its formation.

To impart the stamp of our character upon the blank face of a rock wall on its own

Terms, while retaining our unique personal flair, still remains the *desiderata* of most

Who venture to climb it; by bringing meaning to where there had been only a void is the

Greatest tribute we can repay to nature's clarion call. Let us stay true to the imprint of

History, shun expansion bolts and other contrived ironmongery upon an object that

Still ignites great mystery.

Flow

The Power of Now

To climb one must live as though in a state of nature,
Undistracted by, and oblivious of, the passage of time.
Each moment, each step, occurs in the here and now —
Seared into reality by the intensity of the present.

No sense contemplating the past or predicting the future,
We climbers experience the entire range of emotion by focusing all of
Our perception into the present tense of being, transcendent in its splendor.

Nothing else can possibly suffice than to endure and celebrate these intense
periods of time,
For now we have stepped out of mere time on our own volition,
And passed into a type of suspended animation where
Nothing else counts or occurs except the next step taken now —
Out of the wake we leave behind us.

Our Way to the Top

Alone I drift in visions of peaks;
Alone I grasp the arrogance of feats
Done so brusquely, and without any uncertainty,
As if to mock my reverential devotion to glories won by serendipity.

I revel in that special quality of the uncertainty of the outcome,
Regardless of skill, that is experienced during the bond of indulging
Ourselves in the useless and dangerous sheer joy of climbing,
With the reward for success being achievement of that peculiar harmony of ceaseless
Flow and feedback of triumph over problems, one after another, *seriatim.*

Mirabile dictu, it's the successful process, then, and not the result,
That most rewards our efforts no matter how difficult;
I have thus become what I am doing—an existential reality where becoming
is entangled with being.

The experience of competent flow from one problem to the next effectively makes all
Our actions merge with our self-consciousness
Scrambling together our sense of self with our own actions,
'til it's impossible to conceive of one without the other in juxtaposition.

Thus we banish feelings of futility by setting up a problem that does have a solution, but
Is conditional: for we will have placed ourselves in a precarious situation that can be

Retrieved only by yet more hazardous action—or else we are not to achieve the Contentment of beings whose willfully directed motions render all our endeavors Transcendent, correct, and far-reaching.

Are we then no more than action-addicted creatures of habit?
No—because we find ultimate *meaning* in the process of just becoming into being—
Where reaching the summit virtually crystallizes the effort that has necessarily achieved
That success, and symbolizes perfection, standing in mute testament to all our sincere efforts —
Despite our defects, deficiencies, and raw dread—that
We have not lost our way on the trip to the top.

Awe and Wonder

The Journey and the Destination

Ever beckoning me toward your perfect acme,
Your top is not that which I seek for myself; instead, it's the vision of
Your unravished purity tainted merely by my presence that I can't
Ultimately erase from my brain and which consumes my soul,
And is that which lures me ineluctably upward to that obscure apex of your
earthly zenith.

Once achieved, the fever's snapped, for now I know what others do not;
That I've endured the mindless slog and made the supple moves required
to penetrate
Your recondite sanctum, unbeknownst to the multitude who can only stare
in wonder at your
Imposing presence—never to know or experience the sacrifice of the body
And the withering of the soul required to stand silently serene on your
arcane summit.

Truly, then, the journey is part of the destination, if not its greater half, one
that entails sacrifice:
For to travel to a location is merely to move from here to there—
But to sacrifice one's body and mind in the pursuit of an inchoate, abstract
object
Strikes bewilderment, even fear, into the very marrow of the casual
observer's bones
And brings to fruition the nascent, yet ever-widening breach between the
initiated
Who have experienced the *ne plus ultra,* and the multitude that has not.

Wonder and Embrace

Billowing white crystals spin off your summit,
Swirling about in a gyrating pattern,
Lenticular drifts lost to time, motion in perpetuity,
World without end, unless it be mine.

After numbing hours of plodding along the approach march
I turn a sharp bend—and first behold your magnificent bulk abruptly
Zoom into focus, and strike me dumb with awe
Leaving me gobsmacked in wonder by the astounding challenge:
Is *that* what I'm to surmount? Is *that* what I'm to scale? Is *that* where my
ambition draws me nigh?
Ah, the lure of these big things and the insignificance of my form
Humble me astonishingly more than your massive, silent presence could
ever do alone!

Upward, onward, face to the sun —
As reflected off your glistening mantle of ice,
Yet still searing my eyes through double lenses:
Am I to continue, though partly snow-blind?

A ledge is reached that holds but one foot over another, one at a time;
No room for faltering laces as crampons bite into gritty snow;
One slip, one tangle, one snarl away from the eternal void
We creep along, one by one where another one had stayed.

A sharp crack is heard not too far away, and a rumbling follows:
You eject your imbalanced snow with astonishing forces
At 40, 50, 60 miles each hour 'til I can't possibly know;

I idly wonder if the force that created you
Also created me: Were we made for each other
Though fashioned out of such different clay?
No matter now, for I am locked in your embrace
Bound to finish or be erased.

Alan V. Goldman

My Soul Lures Me Higher

Mountain, mountain in the night
Looming o'er our tiny perch
Such a wonder, such a sight
We cling to you, though in the lurch.

Mountain, mountain, you are arrayed
With knife-edged ridges in a row
And how we struggle not to be swayed
By your crevasses that come and go.

What majesty awaits next morning's glimpse
Of your strongholds beneath the summit;
Your *gendarmes* and cornices that must be "cinched"
Make us weary, wary, and wise, to wit:

None do chance the morning's fluffy snow
Nor do any attempt to negotiate
A route that might be safer below
Lest they fall prey to hidden crevasses that satiate

Your hunger for those who mock your interdict,
And your avalanches that take one and all;
Yet upwards I, myself, must still go, for something clicked
Inside my soul that lures me ever higher, no matter how hard the fall.

Last Leg of the Trek to Kilimanjaro's Kibo Hut

I plodded through a desolate place: a parched, vast expanse of seeming infinity, studded
with ancient volcanic ejecta of igneous boulders, both huge and small, both smooth and irregular.
The peculiar flora of the lower regions, like the giant groundsels and lobelias, are long gone—ever since passing the sign below, some time ago, posting: "Last Water".

Though "only" about eight miles in length, the broad expanse, denuded of vegetation, seemed almost boundless, except for the distant, beckoning lure of hulking Kibo Peak itself, with its snow-white topped mass looming at the far end of the volcanic desert region, which at least provided some perspective to our plodding advance across that almost devoid moonscape plane.

The altitude, now well above 14,000 feet, began to make itself a factor in my length of stride and depth of breath, as I struggled to adapt to the daytime's searing heat. After about three hours, our group was strung out all across the plane, the bulk traveling at the pace of the slowest hiker, while others more fit prominently strode in front—though we all eventually, after nine hours in total, had reached the Kibo Hut, 15,520 feet, at the base of the volcano. Finally, we had indeed reached the volcano itself, which we had so long thought of in fond anticipation of this transitory moment. This was to be our last refuge, where we'd sleep a bit before setting out on a headlamp-lit ascent to the volcano's rim, almost 4,000 feet higher at a steep angle. A scree-type slog of immense proportions awaited us.

The crossing of the volcanic expanse made me feel as though I was being ritually purified through pain, before becoming allowed to attempt the ascent of this quasi-sacred peak: it was the volcano's last moat of defense against violation by any random wanderer.

Only the most determined climber could conceive of daring to cross this bleak region of silence where neither fauna nor rustling vegetation is to be heard, and with clouds rolling along the volcanic plane.

Some of our eyes by now had acquired the thousand-yard stare; we all looked gaunt and a bit pale, but still perky, infused with nervous energy, though drained of ordinary vitality; manifestly, we were pumped up by an adrenaline rush that drove our bodies to perform to exhaustion *after* having spent what seemed our utmost ounce of strength. The feeling while crossing the volcanic desert was one of quiet, intense desperation, for each person knew that if one ever stopped one would be essentially marooned as in a desert, waiting until some rescue workers could reach us.

So we had met our match just in getting to the base of the peak in order to do the climb we had so long anticipated; what's more, we had come to terms with ourselves, or at least I had, feeling fragile, but still agile, having lost weight and strained to a point almost beyond exhaustion. We had become acquainted with ourselves in a manner not easily achieved through even the most arduous training exercise program, where one can stop and use a towel to wipe the sweat off, and gulp at the watercooler. The only water we had was what we carried with us in our Nalgene bottles—there was no Camelbak of water then on the market that we could have used to sip water at will without any effort, and *without stopping*. And stopping was what we were most adjured *not* to do by our guides, who encouraged us to proceed slowly but steadily without taking too many water breaks. Moreover, my water itself was saturated with tetraglycine hydroperiodide, in tablets dissolved long ago, giving the water a chemical taste with the medicinal smell of iodine.

Thus, I had attained access to my inner self, which drove me on despite the sweaty shirt and parched throat. I had met the "enemy," and he was us, as the saying goes, or rather "he was always within us," to be more precise—my strained limitations defining the scope of my being.

Awed Humility

Your majestic wall of alpine splendor momentarily freezes our will to strive;
Leaping up from the high plains in an angry-looking thrust, craggy, stolid, yet seeming alive,
With the spirit of the mountain gods circling your top in a wreath of mist,
Onward we push past your looming mountain wall, aiming for a tryst;
But nature seems to have so shielded you from such unwelcome intruders as we
Who seek only to share your view over the plains more than 3,500 feet below so that we can see
Just how puny we must be to you, secure in your stronghold of boulders and scree.

We take the path of least resistance, a basin and *couloir* littered with alpine debris,
That leads up toward your summit ridge, a different challenge to be treated all its own
That calls forth the adventurer in us to tiptoe past your spires and never to groan
As we slither our lithe forms between your ever-sharp *aiguilles*, like threading a fine needle encompassing
Your splendid isolation from the sight of humans, who look as though they have no understanding.

Nothing more of how jealous are we of your perch atop your fortress of mountain formations 'til we reach the place that constitutes your summit and provides us stupendous

Comprehension of the vista on which we all carry on below, as if nothing is overlooking

It silently, with patches of glistening, clinging snow, festooning your summit in

Seeming defiance of gravity, tugging it far, far below; we thus attain your hard-won

Summit in a spirit of awed humility.

On the Continental Divide

Trudging, trudging alone in despair,
We see a glimpse of an expanse of air;
A bowl so deep it looks like a loop the loop.

A herd of your mountain goats sternly observes
Us from a far ridge in this, their sanctified preserve.
We go around a hillock of driven snow,
Then your form appears to us in a glow.

Backlit by the pre-dawn blueish tinge of the sun's iridescent aurora,
None can escape the feeling that we are entering into your aura
Hidden away *in mysterium tremendum,* the Continental Divide!
We gently prepare to meet your sanctum at the edge on this side.

Then we scale your slope that splits the waters open wide
Agog at the twin peaks that loom above and block our vision of ranges far
afield.
We focus intently on Grays' Peak (14,270 feet) cast in classic pyramidal sides
The mountain goats now taking little heed of us for we have passed by their
ridge's slope.

Atop the summit on the Continental Divide, we see the Front Range of mountains
Close beside, and in the far distance we apprehend the vast scope of nature's
upthrust
Perturbation along the nation's backbone, stretching hardly constrained
Throughout the wilderness that exists, and shatters without feeling much of
its crust.

A Complicated Relationship Bathed in Wonder

Mountain, mountain there you be:
Your eternal presence always pursuing me.

It perplexes me that I'm alive, and thus so mortal,
While you are utterly inanimate, but are and will be extant
For indeterminate millennia, as though untouched by the passage of time.

How can I navigate in your harsh conditions, my being only that of flesh and bones,
In stark contrast to all your sharp scree and virtually infinite array of unstable, jagged talus stones?

Surely my quest to attain your summit
Must have revealed my flawed
Attempt to use you as a test of my limit;

I must appear in your majestic amphitheater of snow and rock bands enveloping your slopes, majestic beyond compare;
However, I will remain merely a transitory mortal, no matter how I may strive to flaunt my deeds in an arrogant display, as if on a dare;

By and by, all my efforts will nonetheless be lost to time (unless some route or mountain feature be named after me so that my legacy carries on):

But the mountain's enduring presence simply arrests the progress of time:
There's no "before, during, and after" in its conception of the world;
It merely exists perpetually in the present, in the here and now, for each and every second of time.

The passage of time and the brevity of life, however, are clearly perceived by mortal eyes;
As the Renaissance French poet Francois Villon famously asked, "Where are the snows of yesteryear?" ("*Mais ou sont les neiges d'antan!*") (from the "*Ballade des Dames du Temps Jadis*"), to emphasize the impermanence of our conditions and the finite nature of life.

So each person climbs his or her own mountain, striving to impart meaning to both the mountain's presence, and to the frail human condition, which is made all too manifest while we struggle on your sharp ridges for our destiny.

These are the kinds of notions that rattle my brain
As I strive to comprehend the nature and quality of my climb
In relation to my resources, the forces of fate,
And the mountain's wondrously silent and ever-brooding presence.

Moonlit Mountain

Mountain, mountain, your ice glistening white,
Shimmering with the glow of perpetual light,
Quietly shining on a Moonlit night —
How did your sheen so envelop my senses?
How did my seeing your glimmering reflection
Blind me to your hidden majesty of solitary seduction?

Were you thus made for no one to behold your arcane grandeur?
Or were you designed for Seekers such as we to wilt at your
wondrous display
Of alpine purity, of essential untold privacy?
Nothing I bring can add to your splendor,
Which makes me no more than an idle onlooker.

Mountain, mountain, your soaring sight
Makes me quake and tremble at your might;
Jealously guarding your stupefying heights
From all those not prepared to witness
Something hidden deep within your primal form:

The trace of a sweeping brush leaving a sign of the
Creation's origin —
Hardly to be glimpsed among our world's common detritus
Of sodden earth and mundane vision.

And with open eyes along your ramparts,
I see that the whole earth is full of the glory of Creation
Of which you are but a fragment and I a speck —

Though I alone am instilled with the presence of mind
That makes me see you as you appear:
Neither good nor evil,
But just that you are "there," as Mallory famously quipped,
And so pose a challenge to my ego to surmount
Your heights and vainly claim them for my own.

On Being and Intent

Alone I struggle in a desolate place,
Freely confined in an infinite space;
Slowly, slowly I do progress —
Till there's nothing left but for me to profess:

That you *do* loom above the valley floor
Like some sinister and stultifying dream of your
Casting a shadow over those who would seek for more —
A harsh, hostile-looking, towering peak
That exerts its malignant-seeming presence
Upon all those who would dare to seek to do true penance:

For I am humbled and broken by your sheer mass and expanse,
And because I never accounted for your encompassing grasp
To stifle me, at the very moment of my success,
But, banish such feelings, for "that way madness lies" (*King Lear*, Act III,
Scene 4, Line 21)

In that thinking along this path would lead one to ascribe to your actions
A terrifying self-awareness of the impact of your own presence, and
That you do *know* you exist, and thus would be a virtually sentient being
That seems able to discern the nature and consequences
Of its actions, and so must possess a knowledge of
Right from Wrong, and in particular,
An awareness of my desperate distress.

No—despite the seductive drive to impute intent to the mountain's varied actions,

Despite its seeming, sometimes, to mock all our striving,

When people merely climb mountains, they dispel any notion of

A mountain being a "being";

Thus, climbing a mountain affirms humanity's uniqueness in knowing Right from Wrong

By placing mankind wholly apart from the stage upon which we may, admittedly, be driven to

Act out our exploits, and by demonstrating mankind's perverse free will

To go deliberately where nature does not support our thriving.

Idealized Perfection

My eyes leaped upward across your seamless, sweeping symmetry
To the point where your soaring peak vanished far beyond the clouds,
almost mercifully,
Hidden from prying eyes that would subject your shape to brutal trigonometry
For assessing your summit's height relative to other points of virtual infinity,
While I sat below in rapturous wonder at your naked form's brazen intrepidity.

Is your random structure shaped only by gravity and pressure, or
Does it conceal within its jagged form some hint of forces yet unknown,
Borrowed from the Creation's *ex nihilo* cryptic design that out of nothing
Is produced something wondrously perfect in its abstract uniqueness?

As I contemplated your initial origin, I pondered my ultimate fate, being
flesh and blood,
And condemned to vanish without a trace, ground into the dust of the ages:
I wonder, is that your journey's end as well, like a living being, to return to
Random, scattered dust amid the perpetual, uncaring, even promiscuous
forces of nature?

Snowbound Giant: Object of My Desire

There it is, a jagged upthrust of the earth's crust;
Its privacy protected by a massive series of hanging ledges clad in snow,
Daunting in its arcane splendor, scoured by sharp sastrugi and narrow flutes
—

Sometimes dotted with granular, fragile rime atop sweeping megabarchan snowdrifts;
I know that I am but a spectator in this, the playground of nature's wildest elemental forces, and the natural environment of the avalanche.

Yet I do persevere, a tiny form inching across the silent snowbanks; silent, except for the howling of the ever-blowing winds that throughout time carved those peculiar snow formations guarding the mountain's flanks.

Ominously, the summit rock nearly pierces a cluster of lazy, lenticular clouds hanging in the sky, presaging precipitation, which can develop into a violent storm.

Employing the rest-step technique with monotonous determination, I make surprisingly steady progress toward the mountain's eerie peak, recondite to all but the most committed of climbers.
Was that what I was? If I "am what I am doing," then, yes; but I know that within my soul I am more than the sum of my accomplishments; I need no activity to define what I am, for I am what I am, my own, personal supreme being, to whom I must sometimes pay humble homage.

Hazards of a Climb

Solitary Motion in the Wake of an Avalanche

Alone I stepped across the windswept, blank horizon,
Devoid of features showing life's once persistent presence,
Negotiating jumbled blocks of churned-up snowpack,
While stumbling through the broken tundra

Where does this bleak prospect abate its oppression?
Where does this receding landscape halt its confusion?
When does life's vitality re-emerge from among the crumpled tree stumps?
When do the cracked boulders cease to litter the forsaken land?

I see only an oozing gash cutting across the once magnificent slopes
Exuding the mountain's excess of imbalanced snow, this, the mountain's
Natural phenomenon for dealing with a distortion of gravity's hold on a
granular sliding surface not fit to grip the weight of its burden of snow and ice
—

Generally thought to lie between 30 and 45 degrees of incline, with 38
degrees being the peak tipping point, or, more cruelly put, "the sweet spot".

But the avalanche is the mountain's cleansing agent, violently shedding
excess snow off of the overburdened land beneath its delicate slopes,
restoring nature's balancing act between the tug of gravity and the weighty
mass of snow it just so holds in place.

So viewed *a la longue*, the avalanche serves a positive purpose of restoring
Balance to nature's grand schema of cladding the slopes with a cover of snow,
Working in harmony with a Grand Design ultimately beyond our mortal,
solipsistic comprehension.

Aftermath of an Avalanche

A crack, and a rumble; a boom, and a tumble,
And all beneath me fell away in a slab-style avalanche,
Never to be caught, escaping all restraints, plowing down
All that stood in its path of annihilation: trees, rocks, and ski-mobiles;
And let's not forget the frame of the solitary skier, tossed about
Like laundry in a dryer; head over heels, face first, then backward
Upward and sideways, but always downward, downward, ever plummeting
Like the rolling stone that gathers no moss and leaves no trace of its existence
Except a nasty scar scraped into the fractured earth.

I'm alive—the first thought that comes to mind; but am I injured too?
No? Then whence do I proceed to extricate myself from my precarious
predicament: up, down, left, right, leeward, windward—all seems jumbled
Far beyond recognition and lacking in any orientation.

Time slows down till it seems to stop; I'm paralyzed with fear lest I go about
and plunge into some newly formed hidden crevasse, or worse yet, trigger
A secondary slide that takes me with it.

But I'm standing, while others lie buried, and so I have a reciprocal duty to seek
out the living from among the dead; peeper peeps, and locator locates in my
Rigorous box-grid search, section by section, ruling out the nothingness
till I come upon a shrill return, and begin digging frantically, downward, ever
downward, seeking signs of movement or noise among the silent, desert-like,
But ruined plain of what was once nature's most graceful slope.

Trapped

Sparkling splendors blinking in the night,
How can they know of our pitiful plight?

We cast our eyes upwards in search of solace,
But we know we're trapped out on the lip of this
Lengthy cornice.

One ponderous move backwards and we risked all
By triggering the overhanging, unsupported outcrop
Of compressed snow — so delicate we now barely
Dared to crawl —

Frozen in fear lest our creeping cause a
Precipitous, fatal fall, and thus become our
Own springboard propelling us to the unknown
Other side.

So we crumpled in terror at our self-made
Predicament 'till we unashamedly cried.

Who could save us from our own poor judgment
In striding forward — drenched in *hubris* — drawn on
By the meretricious allure of a shimmering cornice
That stretched out into the boundless blue sky?

A cornice that only *now* we knew it to be, and realized
Threatened to collapse underneath us, for by definition
It wasn't supported by the rock of the mountain such that
We would be mortally imperiled by the pressure of but one
Fateful step that could plunge us to our doom.

So we winced when we cast our eyes upwards, but
There was no refuge there:

Only *inside* us could there be the noble humility that
Would enable us, God willing, to
Enter that special space reserved for those who
Undertake a search for redemption,

And were thus willing to wriggle backwards on their bellies —
Without any appeal to a self-serving, saving form of
Grace.

Swinging Pendulum Traverse

Jamming halfway into an off-width crack,
I reach for an arm bar with my body sideways,
Wedged in securely, while always applying counterpressure,
for I dare not hammer in a piton here that would mar
Your pristine features.

Pressing against the crack's opposing walls
Heel-toe jams set my path
'til nature here has run its course;
This line's end fast approaches.

My only resource is to traverse your expanse
To find a ledge—this time leading to the very end of your daunting course.
Running across my pendulum path on your near-vertical slope
Picking up momentum as I swing to and fro
With ever larger, faster leaps of faith
In my belayer and his bombproof anchor set above!

Reaching each time for the new route
That would take me up your flat-face wall,
Straining harder to achieve a grip on your edge
That would permit me to ascend my struggle's aim
On a rocky ledge; but halfway there,
I dare to think of the summit.

But I'm being swung too far out of my pendulum traverse's arc, so
That I smash into an arete, a rock spire, behind me that was not in my arc.
Yet delirious with sheer exhaustion from my exhilarating travails
It is no matter that the arete has cleft in twain
My backpack, which has saved the day:
It alone is split in two, though
My jellied back will long feel the impact,
But in just a few more short pitches I'll be not too short of my goal.

O summit, summit, you are mine —
But what have I conquered that's not truly mine?
I conquered only what I'd brought myself:
My fears of failure now dropped away
Like fuzzy dreams that do not stay.

The only thing proved was my showing to one and all
That the limits I had set were a might bit small.
The cliff is passive—a vehicle for my vainglory
To show you what I can do in relying on nothing but my vanity.
As Mallory said, "I conquered only what was in myself, no less, no more."

And the mountain cliff remains serene, still luring climbers to their dreams.
As for me, I promptly collapsed into a gurney for my back
But as the sayings go, "nothing ventured, nothing gained"
For only "he who dares wins"—if at all.

Adventures After Being Gobsmacked in Wonder

Out of the basin we scrambled with glee,
Toward the first rock band and over its scree.
Across the first snowfield we gingerly stepped
Until reaching the second rock wall, which clearly was cleft

Just in twain, just enough for slipping by its bulk,
Then reaching the second snowfield with time enough to sulk,
For it led nowhere but to the base of the peak's north wall:
An impossibly unstable, rotten mass of jumbled rockfall
Looming above us protecting the peak,
So then we traversed to the northwest snowbank in a pique
For now we must lean on our ice axe's shaft
Just to cling to the arching north ridge, which made no one laugh.

Slowly but steadily we inched below the north ridge
Until we ran out of space in which to plant our ice axe's shafts on the last
ledge;
Clearly the crux of the climb was at hand —
Scaling the north ridge itself just to reach a place to stand!
Awkwardly sometimes we stretched out our limbs
Reaching for something to grip in our hands,
To prepare us to mount stoutly on our legs along the summit ridge
Finally gaining purchase enough to stretch one hand to another's as if in a
bridge.

Finally reaching the summit trail, narrow but stable
We strode along jauntily approaching our goal, yet in a rope
So taut that if one fell, others might follow if the belay anchor didn't hold.
But then we knew what it was to be free—*montani semper liberi*—and for
me not to fold!

As I deliberately walked in my usual rest step, I found myself at the top by
almost a misstep;
What was conquered was all beneath me now as we shook hands on the
summit in lockstep,
And all that remained to be mastered was what I had myself brought all
along —
So what have I surmounted? And from what am I free?
Everything!—but my own flaws, wrongs, and fears now buried deep inside
of me.

New Plans

Alone I wandered into an alpine meadow
Across a slope of vast expanse;
Above me loomed the mountain peak
That serenely dominated the sky and all below —
Until I spied a notch above that broke the
Mountain's total coverage of the snowfield at its feet;
Terrain markers on the ground indicated trouble ahead, *i.e.,*
After peering through my Steiner field glasses,
A casting appeared of a slightly dimpled shadow on the field,

Which turned out to be a slow-moving glacier,
complete with crevasses, a
Bergschrund and all;
It was then I realized what hazardous ground I had happened upon
In my jaunty saunter through the back-country;
I had a 1:50,000 climbing map at my disposal, but I carelessly hadn't been
disposed to look,
And thus did not see the jagged, wavy lines indicating the glacier country that
Was narrowly spread out in front of me…

Self-rescue gear from a glacier fall, like prusik knots and climbing web,
was not
Prepared in my gear, and so I turned about, retracing my steps, expanded
wide in the afternoon snow.

Discretion is the better part of valor, or so the hoary maxim goes, and I felt

No pressing need to test my luck, at least not this day—for nothing worthy was at stake,

Hence I felt no shame at all in deliberately, but swiftly, glissading directly out of there!

Am I timid or prudent in my steps?

The glory of it is that no one would receive *that* phone call—at least not on that day.

Success with minimal exposure to unavoidable danger…I drew my line where I found

Solace in the knowledge that I had the instincts of when to take a risk, and of when the

Better part of valor is to hold fast, or retire, when circumstances objectively insist.

Lost Hope: Deciding Whether to Cross the Line, Past the Point of No Return

As I applied my crampon snowshoe technique walking *en canard* like a duckling —
Learned but a week before—and keeping my feet well apart so as not to entangle myself
In a clumsy, slashed-up, bloody heap resembling the hastily discarded *impedimenta* of war,

It was then that I first caught a fleeting sight of the summit that undulating terrain and
Mist had veiled; a chilling vibration now ran up and down my spine in fearful waves,
Which inevitably drew me toward a cabin door of deceptive allure,
The winds at least, in a climber's hut/*refugio* put there for posterity, its inside walls
Covered in last goodbyes, and all those maudlin things…

Then, I drew my conclusions for the next day's journey very carefully, for at these
Altitudes it is known to science that hypoxic euphoria so insidiously erodes the higher
Mental faculties, and the reptilian brain-functions come all too unconsciously to the
Fore, mixed together with a toxic mélange of overly exuberant emotion, distorted

Analysis, and false, hollow pride. To me, this was not the sport of climbing, but a manic

Leap into hazards known, unrealistic talk I say, for we had planned another route down below.

Someone in my group began to speak unrealistically about the distances and terrain

That we must "perforce" cross before noon the next day. I shuddered in fear that one by

One we were *all* slowly "losing it" in the vernacular of our day—that is to say our

Tenuous grip on reality was slipping away day by day, just as our slender contact with

Reality waned appreciably with every boot step sucking us upward toward the sky.

Was this, then, to be our journey's end, to travel across hazards of all kinds: sudden

Rock-fall, yawning crevasses, and exposure to bitter venturi-like winds that sweep

Around the base and face of the mountain like a circular jet stream? And to brave all of

this merely so we could travel the hypotenuse of a giant triangle instead of more safely

Negotiating the shorter legs of the design, as we had planned?

No—I said inside myself, having glimpsed the fate before me just in time to disengage

From a purblind death march into a *direttissima*, which was now presented to me as if it

Were an inevitable feature of a preplanned design in the context of an enjoyable

Adventure sport. So, NO, not this trip, I barked aloud so all could hear. If they survived

And reached the summit, and returned safely to the flatlands, then all manner of glory would

Be heaped upon them, and I branded a coward. I reconciled myself to this outcome, for

Life is too precious a gift to risk knowingly in a gambler's foolhardy bid to dare the

Elements in an exercise of naked vainglory—which could be perceived by anyone, if

Unclouded by a cataract of hubris-like film subtly coating the lenses of the eye.

In the event, which hardly matters in the choice I then had to make, the party that

Pushed on returned after having gone a bit more than halfway, with frostbitten fingers,

toes, and noses, as well as frozen limbs and all the rest. They could forever croon in

hushed tones that they had "at least tried," but I knew better: there had never been any

chance for success with minimal exposure to unavoidable danger… I drew my line

where I found solace in the knowledge that I had the instincts of when to take a risk,

and of when the better part of valor is to hold fast or retire.

Alan V. Goldman

Confronting Fear

The Desiderata That We Climbers Seek

If you seek it in the night,
It will dodge you with a fright.

If you seek it by the light of day,
It won't dwell long enough to be and stay.

Steadily, the crux is drawing nigh
Anticipate it if you can try.

But all I know is that in the crux so dwells
The fear, the trembling, not so well.

To face that challenge head-on clear
Requires more groaning than I can stand to hear.

For it's not the crux itself that we seek,
But the will to surmount it: is it fearful and weak?

Ah, my shadow follows behind
To mock me every time I find
The grit to persevere with those conditions,
Which were made to prey upon my inhibitions.

Early Winter Winds

Vertiginous virgin standing tall;
How do I deal with you, if at all?
Roaring, raging, whipping winds,
Do you cloak yourself where intruders fall?

Twisting, splitting every tent
None do escape your violent rent.
So I burrow myself deep in snow,
Proof against your virulent "No"!

Do I sense a coming pause?
Or am I breaking all the laws
That govern your eternal bulk
And make it proof against all folk?

I wait out your unseasonable, month-early gale
While others strive to move—but only flail.
By and by your storms relent,
And provide me passage where none left went.

Did I overstep something unwary,
Closed to others by your boundary?
But your tower and I have merged forever:
So let none say that "we" were never.

Ice Climbing in Box Canyon

Little by little I improve my rhythm
To achieve a synchronous flow of my limbs in coordinated motion, as if in
a resonant mechanism
While two ice tools and rigid 12-point crampons sink in deep.

I reach for the next level with second crampon hanging in space
As I propel myself upward, as if in vertical ballet, by leg motion always,
for no one
Can *pull* oneself upward by upper body strength alone.

I'm cloaked by my Petzl full-body suit and helmet for climbing
Seat and sternum harness attached by a rewoven (doubled) figure-eight knot
to a locking carabiner
Fixed into a hollow ice screw lodged deep into the bluest ice, which secures
me for now,
Unless the whole shelf shears off and cracks up, like smashed dinner plates,
and chucks
Me aloft. God help me, for then I am lost.

I stretch, fully committed to my route, which is a bold *direttissima,*
Wholly oblivious of the wall's natural formations, eschewing all manner of
natural
Placements and protections, if not in a *direct line straight* to the summit. I'm
Determined to lurch forward by the straightest route to the extent possible
regardless of discomfort.

Will I prove the folly of humans in defying nature to impose our own command?
Or will I falter and take natural variations that can be negotiated, if done in slow trepidation?

Measure by measure I inch up the wall—actually, part of a frozen waterfall of dubious
Coherence and intrinsic strength. I redouble my efforts to seek out a proper place to
Imbed my next hollow ice screw up above the last placement, locking carabiners into the screw,
And hoisting myself up by a push of one leg followed by all the rest,

Til finally reaching the top at last; I'm gleeful, yet subdued by the knowledge that things
Didn't go awry, as they are so inclined to do, infuriatingly, at any time, any place, and for
No reason why…

What do my vicissitudes matter now that I'm safe—if only to show how life itself is all
But a gambler's game with an advantage to the house?

The climb compressed a lifetime into inches and
steps, and laid out a pathway for my
Brash success. Does this mean I should cut corners in my professional life on my way
To the top, or would the guilt and shame, in this context, overwhelm my conscience so
That I heard that "still, small voice" rebuking me from taking an ill-gotten place?

Bailing Out on Twining Peak

Approaching the North Wall of my nemesis just as the pre-dawn light emerged
to illuminate the Wall's fluted chutes and narrow gullies—in this case, at about
4:45 A.M.—I gazed upward, already running my eyes along the ice wall's ridge,
Looking for points of exit so as to be ready to escape the incline when it reached
beyond 75 degrees near the summit's apogee.

With horror, and innermost secret relief, did I realize that the shafts of my brace
of ice tools,
Which allowed me to hang from my well-placed swings planted securely but not
Too deeply, were not ergonomically curved *enough* so as to give my knuckles
sufficient clearance when pounding upward; thus, I was already bested by this
ice wall's hollow, ice-cream scoop's gash, and yet continued striving mightily
not to show my thoughts of terror, and shame, to the world beyond my scope.

Sensing hesitation in my every command: "on belay," "slack," or "tension," my
Rope partner began to doubt my commitment to reach for the summit. Indeed,
when my chance came, I deftly made my exeunt for the ridge—called "bailing
out"—with the lame excuse of "Equipment failure," for it was inconceivable to
admit my true inner dread.

In cruel irony, I did my very best climbing of the day when I sprinted for
the ridge,
Going wholeheartedly gung-ho, fluidly moving to reach my place of safety off
of the wall!

Confidence bests cowardice every time it's given the chance; but only experience can give one the confidence to know the extent of one's capacity; until then, ignorance rules with its ally, fear; no wonder, then, I so expertly gave myself no chance to fail.

The Moment of Decision

Plodding along on the approach march I went,
Ready for whatever thing that would try to prevent
My determined ascent to the top of my peak;
So I trekked along until I saw a long, winding ridge that was not for the weak.

Carefully stepping among the loose scree and sharp talus stones,
I crept along steadily, until reaching a high pass, after about 1,700 yards,
That forked northeast for almost 900 more, to reach my peak's summit ridge
Where I abruptly confronted a gully halfway across to the summit, making me feel
Where is the bridge?

Do I have the temerity to cross this exposed void; are my skills sufficient
to cope with this risk? I judged the situation with my knowledge of hiking
steep slopes; here
The crumbling exposure was daunting as I found myself climbing un-roped
hand over hand,
traveling like a disk;
But confidently secure in myself, I dared the mountain gods to do whatever
they may wish—
Until I finally reached the other side of the gap in the ridge that led cleanly
to the summit finish.

Anxious Doubt

Struggling against the tugging pull of the ever-tightening harness and belay rope,
I suddenly realized that my anchor above was in jeopardy, slowly slipping loose from above, sliding upward while out of sight;

So, I was *not* affixed to a bombproof, stable tree stump after all, but my baseline ropes were yawing and *inching up* the short stump—all just before being ready to let go entirely over the top of the stump, sending me hurtling to my demise too many feet below;

Where was the tipping point before which I could still stabilize the rope's slippage along the length of the stump?
Would I reach the top of the ledge before the ropes came undone and did me in?

My eternity flashed before me, hanging uncertainly in a moment of time:
I was in a race—would I finish the ascent before my protection self-destructed?

And, to boot, I was beset by moments of bitter self-recrimination: had I rashly picked a stump too short for safety's sake, just to make the climb possible from that aspect of the wall to slake my vanity?

In the event, all came right, and the moment of danger passed uneventfully, secretly, known but to me and my inner voice. I had gotten away with it. But the memory of that moment was seared into my mind, if always self-protectively (that is, of my ego) pushed to the very bottom of my thoughts.

Disaster Viewed from Afar and Near

We sallied forth to do battle with our fear;
We were nearly deaf to harbingers of failure,
For we held our future o so preciously dear;

So we had no clear thoughts, and pressed our luck
Far beyond the strength of our gear;
Which duly sheared off the wall to which
We had so carefully prepared to adhere.

To us, blinded by *hubris*, we subsequently consoled ourselves
That **no one** could have had the ear to hear
When the turn of the ice-screws had begun to veer
Askew deep inside the blocks of blue ice into which
Some were penetrating at a faulty angle — off the tier
Of visible striations merely by millimeters —

Except for the most prescient of seers.

The Lure of the Big Mountains

Shambala

I lift my eyes to the hills to give me perspective:

That we are ever challenged by the something further and hereafter;

In this world of finite space, can't there be a hiding place for the divine quality of grace?

Can there ever be the obscure mountain rings of Shambala in the folds of time and space

That we have yet to plant our feet atop their peaks in triumph?

Wreathed in snow around the eight great petals that form an opaque mist,

They all still do lure us on to find this mythical kingdom of bliss.

Call it what you will but know well that there'll always be more Seekers after the peaks wreathing Shambala in pure and permanent snow.

To save for human imagination—that "something else" that calls for exploration;

Striving always to find the next and most distant summit so high that no birds sing.

So onward, onward inside our brains is the quest thus maintained

For the magical mountain of our souls.

Like Alexander may have thought when reaching the Sogdian Rock with

All India beckoning below,

Is this then to be my "journey's end"—no further to explore and go find the fabled peaks of Shambala? At this seeming terminus some legends say he wept; for him, "there were no more worlds to conquer".

Nor more peaks to wrest away from their lonely isolation;
Only exhaling breath for there's at last no reason to hold it fast within his mortal form.

A balloon deflated is a sorry sight to see, its wonder all but gone;
And despair crept into the ranks, for despite having climbed the Rock they feared there would be no more peaks to draw them on.

The Rapture of the Heights

Clothed in your mantle of perpetual snow,
Concealing fissures and crevasses that I cannot know,
Why do you beckon me to scale your cornices
Where fate robs me of all my devices?

A game of Blind Man's Buff you tempt me to dare
Without any remorse for your just being "there."
So why does your siren call so trouble my soul
With visions I know to be false?

Vainglory distorts my perceptions of risk and loss,
So vitiating my mind's better sense of the cost.
A wise fool of a climber I think that I am,
Wholly enraptured by the lure of your scam;
Yet no better, nor worse than the next one's will to be grand.

My trek to oblivion before me lies
That tells all others whose will would be wise:
Hypoxic euphoria being insidious as it is —
The rapture of the heights drains my judgment:
"This is no world for men," as Kipling wrote in *Kim*.
But still I go for I'm content, even ecstatic, never to know it.

Ascent of Mankind on Mountain Ground

Mountain, mountain, glistening white
In a sea of shimmering light.
Why is your presence so alluringly tight?
How did you upthrust just so right?

Faces, ridges, gullies, and moraine
Are just so perfect in their own domain.
When did that which made your reign
Think at all of humans and their pain?

Snow-blind, frostbitten, and starved for air,
My hypoxia-induced euphoria still draws me to your peak's lair
Unrelenting in my steps, I do not think that it is fair
That you remain all-too-serene, without a care;
Nor that your existence is unperturbed, even while you subtly snare,
And while my struggle goes on and on, judgment so impaired.

The Lure of the Summit

I ventured with my team amidst the rugged peaks, after having
Contemplated my challenges on this side of being—without crossing over
to the other;
What were we to conquer and survive to tell the tale
Of our fallen idol—and what indeed will we have vanquished
In such an endeavor? *"None but ourselves,"* as Mallory wryly remarked;
What will I feel, standing on a summit for a brief moment of "glory"?
What will I actually now possess, once I arrive at the top?
Is it worth the struggle to reach for the summit? What will I have obtained,
once there?

Of course, I'll have the knowledge of my struggle itself,
And the self-confidence it arouses, but of what else?
For the summit is but an abstract symbol of absolute perfection camouflaged
in rocky
Debris; yet somehow, it beckons me to breach its solitude
So as to mystically merge with the harmony of the natural world—from
which I fear that
Humans have all become alienated.

That's why I feel propelled to go
Where conditions are surely not conducive to the presence of humans;
So as to forge a bond of perfect harmony with the "natural" world,
Which we too often feel is separate and apart from us, in opposition to
ourselves,

As if we were not intrinsically part and parcel of the natural world around us.

The difficulty of climbing to the summit thus serves to make us feel as though

We have always belonged to the natural world that is already actually inside us.

A Case of Possession

We ambled along the valley floor,
Determined to enjoy ourselves,
As though we were not already grimly committed
To "bagging" this recondite peak,
Which I knew from maps and photos just must be
Over there, far above and beyond a series of snowfields
That encircled its fearsome apogee.

We turned 'round a sharp bend in the trail,
It was only then that I first caught sight of the looming peak, nearly 3,500
feet of gain—from the flatlands at its valley base.
Nearly three and one-half Empire State Buildings—thrust above the valley
floor:
Its monstrous bulk below, its acute apex above, its narrow ridges
And expansive north face, all combined to tame the will to surmount its summit;
Now we began to trudge slowly; our chances seemed bleak.

Still, I was young, headstrong and contrary, and plowed through
A snowfield that was just steep enough to slide; no matter, for the moment
of unleashing
its pent-up power is known to no one but the mountain gods.

What was I seeking that so drove me ever upward,
Fixated on violating the mountain's fearsome privacy
With regard only for my self-aggrandizement?

What was the mountain's power of attraction that
So spurred me on to reach its triangular peak?

Like a child staring at candy on display behind glass,
I wanted to breach the mountain's protection, to possess the mountain's essence,
Which was its summit, where I could sign the mountain's logbook, its register of fellow sojourners;
As if like a lawyer to claim some right of property and abstract possession.

It was only long after I descended
That holistic enlightenment finally came to me:
All this was a case of not only my possessing the mountain,
For I inwardly came to realize that, all along, it had been simultaneously possessing me.

A Curious Relationship Between the Perceiver and the Perceived

Alone I strode toward a promontory very steep;
"There's nothing down below that can't be found up here for us to keep,"
They said, but I know that *that's* not true —
For only at the precipice of the jutting promontory
Can I experience the true emotion: that "we" are actually alone and solitary.

Back with the party of fellow Seekers going after the summit
I and all the others strived to seem so self-assured of our strength and merit
In our quest for the ultimate thrill of being where no mortal should.
So onward and upward we tread none too lightly; (I mused that
Simply because I *could* do something was not a sufficient
Reason that I *ought* to or should.)

And how was their quest for the summit so different from my
Peering over a ledge to soak up the vista and feel transcendent?

Gripped by summit fever, many felt a boundless elation that was
No different from what I had experienced out on a jutting ledge of the
promontory.

Upon attaining the summit, all those so affected felt agog at the
Prospect that the world had somehow "changed," and that it was
Now no longer the world as they had known it.

This feeling of being dumbstruck in astonishment, or utterly
Astounded, was no different from my having been "gobsmacked
In wonder" upon first catching sight of my mountain in
Another climb many years ago.

But I discovered the truth then, as I do now: it is not the *world*
That has changed, but rather the *observer,* who has imputed
His feelings to his surroundings; namely, the observed object
Of his desire; only later had I learned that this was a known
Phenomenon called "Transfer of Affect"—a quite pedestrian
misconception.

So now we were enlightened, I wish I could say, because our
having reached the summit had changed it *in no way*; rather
it was *we* who were changed, and are perpetually changing,
In our endless pursuit of the ultimate truth—of which a mortal
Being can know nothing.

Frustration at the Foot of Forbidden Peak

A journey too far for the likes of my legs,
A destination too remote for the likes of my spirit,
A goal too obscure for the likes of my mind,
An end too bitter for the likes of my soul.

What comes of my sojourn to this wall of ice-clad rock?
Is there no pity for the broken of heart?
What deed of daring-do is required to reclaim
My personal stake in pursuit of success over this soaring

Citadel scraping at the edge of the sky, straining the reach of my eye,
This monolith of infinitude that remains pristine in its solitude —
For no one the likes of me dares to mount an assault on its ferocious privacy:
It remains a solitary spire immune to struggles of the multitude;

And as the mountain gods know,
It will never be more serenely exquisite than it is just right now,
While we puny persons contemplate the perpetual challenge
It poses to all who succumb to the
Meretricious allure of its ungarnered, innate glory.

Fearsome Peak: North Face

Looming high above the valley floor
Lies the "mountain of mountains" in this region's lore:
The North Face of North Peak comes to the fore —
Its serried defenses defeating many climbers with horrific gore.

Striking out just before the dawn,
We hiked up the basin snow-bowl to the right side of the north wall, where we were drawn
To climb up to the First Snowfield, crossing a bergschrund by ladder, bypassing the First Rock Band, or lower head-wall,
While traversing to the left until below the Central Gully, careful not to slide, crampons biting into the crunchy snow.

Then came the ascent in the Gully, traversing on mixed ground,
Always avoiding rock outcroppings, until arriving at the Second Snowfield, renowned
For its sturdy sun-cup formations, traversing to the right as necessary to breach the Second Rock Band, only
To arrive at the *Third* Snowfield, which we traversed as well, this time to the left —

To avoid the most imposing rock-wall of all, the *Third* Rock Band: 60 feet of rotten, sedimentary, crumbling conglomerate, where protection is nearly useless, almost abandoned,
Until our route finally joined paths with the standard North-East Ridge Route, leading directly to an obscure pinnacle, worthy of the misbegotten.

O, if only the mountain could speak! It would reveal the number of its hapless victims lying about,

Crushed by falling rock here, or stumbled off the edge there, or beguiled by a sentinel of slick snow and icy bridges in the belly of the beast's Central Gully route deeply embedded in its North Face;

But the mountain remains indifferent and silent, except for the whipping winds 'round its ridges,

Where some have stepped off the narrow route into a forgotten oblivion,

Despairing of finding meaning and recognition in our quest to climb the daunting North Face.

I cry with bootless bewilderment:

O Lord, what are human beings that you should notice them,
Mere mortals that you should be mindful of them?
For they are nothing more than a vapor, and
Their days are like a fleeting shadow.
(Psalm 144: 3-4; see also, Psalm 8:5; and Psalm 39: 6-7; personal translation)

So the climber sets out with this burden of his insignificance,

And is lured by a desire to imbue his actions with something of value that is inimitable—transcending the confines of time and space in order to

Impress his fullness on the bleak void of the mountain's silent majesty.

To what end does the mountaineer strive to seek out the summit of

Such an obscure object of desire? To show what man is capable of achieving, even in a hostile environment that admits of no allowance for error. To go where his presence was never contemplated or foreseen in the Grand Design of things.

Lost Pinnacle

Thrusting upward like a potent spire,
The gleaming rock-wall lured us to its tower,
Beckoning us with the meretricious allure of its raw power,
Gleaming white in wind-scoured sandstone
Emerging upright from a mantle of some perpetually snow-clad throne.

Would this vertical formation yield to our collective groan
And allow us to enter onto its forbidden zone?
Upward, upward, forevermore, it drew us onward despite brewing trouble,
Dangling the reward of reaching its climax of convergence at its sharp summit where
Stark, clean, bold lines of ascent to its naked pinnacle clearly outlined its grooves, where nothing was gentle or subtle.

Or would it bar our access and send us scrambling down, making us plummet
As we failed to scale its vertiginous flanks, sighing with a pathetic moan?
O yes, it guards its ferocious privacy as though it were inside its own bubble,
As it virtually shook us off its sheer slabs from which we had desperately hung
In hopeful, pent-up anticipation, but without due regard for its minatory
shower of pelting rubble.

Special Conditions

Red Snow

Trekking along as carefree agents,
We pushed on to the base of your summit;
Everything looked ideal, symmetrical and as expected,
Until we saw a red-tinged layer high in your snows.

What could it be, this reddish-pink snow—except an omen for us to go?
But we recalled our experience, melting snow for water even though far below
Yielded nothing but sickness in total free flow.
Warily we ascended with ice axe in hand,

From belay point to point we reached your band of snow.
Where each step smelled putrid and rotten as watermelon mush.
We checked our handbook of your mountain ecology
And we were startled to learn that the ancients had already known of you,
millennia ago.

Our modern science has learned that you are *alive*:
A one-cell alga—*Chlamydomonas nivalis*—living off the Sun,
Photosynthesizing when green in the summer's glow
But lying dormant and red, surviving the cold of three mountain seasons.

Your dormant red cysts then effloresce, and turn green to soak up the summer
sun,
After surviving so long in a state of hibernation.
How empowering it must be to draw upon the source of life itself when you
flow down-slope with melting snow —
A sensation we pondered while treading through your garden.

Why return high again only to suffer from low temperatures and little nutrition

With the source of life at your disposal, we pondered further;

Why lie dormant at all, and live only where life is easier?

But then an ironic thought passed through our brains:

What were *we* doing climbing in your difficult terrain, which is hostile to life,

Yours as well as ours, to be sure, both of us wholly "out of our element,"

Yet enduring the freeze, year after year, only to repeat the cycle forever?

Just how much are we really alike, returning to hardship without a complaint—

No; with contentment in the experience of eternal cycles of dormancy and rebirth,

Your fate is dictated by natural rhythms, while ours is forced upon us by our own "free will…"

Faith and Reality

A silent presence that is always felt
Following our footsteps without a doubt;
A sense of self, and of another
Combine to make us alert and shudder:

Is this presence that is clinging to us here
Really a regret for the isolation we have imposed on ourselves?
Are we not social beings who desire to care,
And do we not think of the unnatural solitude as creating a special bond with all
Those who have also sought for themselves?

The need for companions to accompany us always —
Through moments of peril magnified here by our solitude's gaze
But only ourselves reborn by an inner penance
Purged of undue pride in total self-reliance.

Humbled before the mountain's daunting form
We scramble, we grip our ascenders, figure eights, and slide
On your blank walls, and through your fickle storms,
Transformed are we by your Siren's call, "Come hither".

Trust we must in our own ability

But always tempered by your perceived amenability—

Ah, "perceived" it must be, for we can't project ourselves

Onto your being, which seems as though *jejune*, weighed down by our trivial
banality.

Devoid of emotional reaction, you stand tall for all who seek out themselves

In your icy grip of a perceived challenge that presents itself as a real possibility;

But only when we are purged of gross sentimentality

Will we come into contact with your frightening reality —

Wholly oblivious of our very being —

And of the struggle both with you and within ourselves.

Last Reflections on a Journey to Nowhere

We skied from Aspen along the 10th Mountain Trail,
To Shrine Mountain Inn—what a cozy place to be, with about 30 or so other
skiers,
But I came here for training purposes, to learn enough for
Emergency survival outdoors, unlinked to any pre-made structure.

So we made a "Quinzhee Hut" about a mile due east beyond Shrine Inn;
It's a temporary shelter from the winds, engineered
By excavating a circle around the intended center and
Piling all the snow into the center, so that, once hollowed out, it will be large
enough for two.

The snow dome being completed, we then excavated an entrance with
A right-angled "dock-leg"—
So that winter winds and blowing spindrift could not enter our sleeping quarters.
Another technique we employed was mixing up all the snow so that
Proper "sintering" of the many layers of unequal density would occur
and bolster the structure's integrity.

Our Quinzhee Hut was built high enough to permit our sitting up while in
a sleeping
Bag, and to crouch around, usually sorting gear and food.
Next, we remembered to poke a ski pole several times directly through the
top of

The dome, before the snow-ceiling hardened, so that oxygen could enter and our exhaled
CO_2 would not accrete inside our little fortress of snow.

Next, we smoothed the inside of the dome as much as possible so that any melting snow
Would travel down along the inside edges of the Hut, and not drip down directly onto our heads.

Now that the *mise en scene* was completed, our "survival" skills became further tested.
We started a fire with small propane tanks and cooked up a hearty stew, which tasted like filet mignon after having munched for hours on trail mix—a wholesome but ultimately
Boring assortment of peanuts, almonds, walnuts, sunflower seeds, raisins, and chocolate chips.

So things looked "A-OK," just fine and dandy, 'til winter storms began to blow.
Relieving oneself meant some exposure of naked skin, both front and back, to the nearly
"Flash-freeze" temperature outside, but nature did surely call.

Well, all this was "fun" for a day, but the program course specified, "Three days and three nights…"

Gradually, insidiously, the repetition of stylized moves became a drag on morale; and
The bitter cold, which was at or below 15 degrees Fahrenheit, with steady winds of 20 mph and gusts up to 40, only aggravated our condition to nearly the point of submission.

The cold thus slowly seeped into our bones right through our down jacket's fleece and

High-tech, "wicking" underwear; indeed, it was so cold as to make one feel that one's

Bones would snap if the angle of pressure was just right.

So those are the conditions we endured as part of the training program; I assure you

That by the third day even lukewarm water seemed as tasty as a glass of Cabernet.

Now we were "hard mountain men" for a few days, after returning to Shrine Mountain Inn,

Where we basked in glory, feted by the uninitiated, who listened carefully to our brief,

Three-day sojourn into the backwoods.

In any event, there I had a physical and psychological communion with nature that

Reverberates in me to this very day.

Challenge on Fair Terms

Reflections on Mountaineering, Morality, and Life

As I climb your rugged heap of boulders, unstable ledges, and loose scree
I reflect on the upsurging violence that must have formed your many
layers—the Rockies are "young" mountains in geological time—and are
still rising today, with a millennium of years yet to grow and stay.

If ripping and scraping to the top of your heap was required to form your
ideal
Symmetry, how much *less* are my boundaries capable of worthy success,
relative to
What you have accomplished, inch by inch over eons of time.

I ascend to the top of this, my private junk heap, standing on a summit of
crumbling
Conglomerate—tiny bits of which are compressed by the cold, and tinged
like mortar
Stained with the blood of those who tried and failed to scale your peak.

I am respectful and awed by your emergence from the recondite depths of
some ancient ocean floor —
But what am I to say to myself and the inevitable others when they hound
me about my
Aspirations to a creditable climb?

Mankind's puny aspirations were conceived while purblind in a tunnel vision delimited
By his narrow perception informed only by pure chance—nothing illustrates this more than your presence by chance, without being aware of your selection of rocks to
Upthrust without thought, without will, and, and yet resulting in something of Worth upon which most others may only glance…

As I gaze at the horizon, boxed in three ways by a ring of undulating mountains,
I cannot fail to feel the tugging appeal of scaling one of those peaks to escape from this natural enclosure.

My sights are set on one peak in particular that seems to have a deep notch
Separating it from its adjacent sentinel companion by which I might pass through the ring of mountain walls surrounding this bleak box canyon.

Am I cheating nature's will, exploiting her weaknesses,
Or am I fulfilling nature's expectations of me
By applying my human canniness?

Are the mountains made for me to scale as I would,
Or are they immutable expressions of nature's intention to corral the
Limits of humanity and so stifle my free will?

As I reached toward the notch, I spied a dihedral and also the very place
For me to affix my spring-loaded cams and other ironmongery,
So that passage would be made practicable and safer for the human to work his will.

But then a voice whispers: "*cheater and fraud*"—for me to make of this
Mountain a thing to be dominated by my own free will, cunning, and skill,
Just another obstacle in my rise to the top of my climbing career—threading
the needle
So fine as to make me grasp that the "path of least resistance" is covered in
shame and fear,
For, as Messner might say, not having met the mountain itself on its own
natural terrain;

I now can't truly say that I did even prevail—except if I grimly adhere to a
pure, clean,
Direttissima route so rough such that none can accuse me of having sought
the easiest way out of there.

Challenge on Fair Terms

Shimmering with your coat of ice, reflecting onto high ponds unseen,
Standing silent, still and serene—until you avalanche me in a dream.
Will you let me pierce your fastness, securely fixed by pinnacles like bars?
Or will you defeat my brazen assault upon your majestic mass?
I will not accept a victory granted to the weak, while I gaze beneath the stars
Above your bulging cornices that dare me to your peak;
Fluted chutes of wind-carved *verglas* and snow
speak to me in the silence of those who
Know of how the mountain ensnares.

I know your defenses too well to let me feel I deftly surmounted your
delicate, thin lines,
with heaps of ironmongery at my disposal,
That lead to the summit, bypassing all blockades of rock and mixed terrain;
Crevasses that are virtually bottomless abysses, separated by rock walls and
moraine.
But, like Messner, I want to confront you on fair terms, spared nothing of
the indicia of all your danger signs.

Like Alexander, "I will not steal a victory" won by your misfortune or
circumstance;
Please show me all your bristling teeth so that my expectations
Will not be undone by prevailing only through mere chance;
A test that doesn't challenge the taker isn't worthy of its name, and
Defeats all my fond anticipations.

Nature's Handiwork

O citadel of formidable solitude, why do you burden me so?

Your stronghold remains all too elusive, alone in its stark redoubt;

How can I scale your vertiginous rock walls and elude your snowbanks of serried seracs

When the route to your sublime pinnacle of perpetual ice and snow is obscured by

Serpentine paths leading to that oblivion of which humans cannot know?

I stretch, I contort, I ease my way through your maze of false leads and false summits —

Only to realize that your essential purity is not assailable, barring a small army of

Scaffold-builders who would be climbing only their own handiwork and not your natural features.

Not to deface nature's handiwork, but to adapt to a mountain's features, using only

Basic tools, as Messner boldly proclaims, and so to reach its top is the very *desiderata*

Of true climbing ethics. While resignation to defeat is difficult to absorb, it nonetheless

Entails serene acceptance of nature's sanctity, which is, without a doubt, forevermore.

Rope Partner

Rope Partner of Mine

Rope partner of faith, are you truly mine?

You efficiently observe all technical rope commands,
Such as "on belay," "slack," and "tension."
You cheerfully and fairly exchange the lead with me at the sharp end of the rope,
No matter the pitch's severity, without so much as a grumble;

Yet I still feel a certain distance separating us from the bond of blood brothers.
Would you cut my rope to protect your life, as well as that of others?
Every climber must answer this test within the bounds of his conscience.
"Leave no man behind" is the warrior's claim of devotion to team spirit;
"One for all, and all for one" is the climbing team's unspoken mantra.

But what had been clear is muddied now here, when we find ourselves to be caught up *in extremis.*
Then, morality shifts away from the altruistic, and toward the selfish body-count mindset of crisis management, subjective triage morality, and the "weighing" of the "relative" costs of one's actions.

Relative to what and for whom? And according to what new standards of conduct,
Especially for we who are rope partners, inculcated to expect that a certain measure of
Devotion would always be maintained, but here is now slickly subverted?

Most perplexing is the law that recognizes the time-honored defense of "necessity" or *force majeure*
To allegations of intentional misconduct; does this exculpatory doctrine encompass and subsume our eternal, mutual vows?

What does one person have the right to expect from another in exceptional circumstances,
Where conditions never foreseen render moot that unique bond between us as rope partners?

Character of the Ideal Rope Partner

To stand firmly while the world around you collapses
Is the hallmark of intrepidity and ineradicable commitment,
Stolid, like a mountain in the midst of an earthquake around you,
Ineluctably extruded onto the environs about you that wobble and convulse
While the mountain remains steady in its set place, unperturbed and unrattled.

So, too, do some people persevere in the wake of quavering circumstances
That would stagger others who become unhinged by passing fortune,
Shaking their faith in the natural order of things, while the others remain
steadfast in their loyalty to certain immutable principles that inform their
notion of the world's structure, which does not fluctuate with every passing
disturbance in its surroundings.

Knowledge of the tipping point is found in confident prediction of who will
break up or hold fast in any trying situation: this the mountaineer must discern
in every other person before placing his faith in the hands of another.

Will a person hold together or disintegrate under duress is the perpetual
and iconic question in the selection of a rope partner, whose conduct may
determine the course of another person's life.

Will he stand firm like the mountain in the wake of a tumult, or will he fold
and become like the flotsam and jetsam of every passing storm's whirlwind?

Role of Luck, Fate & Chance

A Meditation on Mountain Whimsy

How shall I judge you, and not you, but me?
Is the flaw in your inanimate face a sign of nature's imperfection,
Or of humanity's superior perception and exploitation?

Your imposing *gendarmes,* barring the straight path to the sky, cannot flee
But only stand idly by while I circumvent them.
What of your knife-edged ridges that one can scoot across while sitting down,
What of your yawning crevasses that I can bridge across without looking down,
Lest their intrinsic pull plunge me to their fathomless depths?

Known but to the mountain spirits that dwell in shame
As climbers scour your every facet, no matter the rock bands, and
Never succumb to despair, for you always present ample ways out of there.
Now how shall I judge you in opposition to me?
Who can pass through the weakest chinks hidden in your armored tower?
But who, like unwelcome intruders, can still be swept away
By your venturi winds blowing hard, then funneling inviting calm
Until the other side is reached
When your power again moves across your face, sweeping us to the four
corners
As if we were nothing but specks of dust?

Lenticular clouds and spindrift off your top presage the next blowing gale,
triggering avalanches of white death;
Who's to claim victory when success is too often measured by unforeseen
luck:
The cornice that didn't collapse, the avalanche that wasn't triggered,
The crevasse that didn't hide under a blanket of snow—are all of little
comfort to those who really know.

A Tribute to Freedom

Covered from the stormy skies
Resting undisturbed,
Until my internal senses tell me something
Is looming over your ridges, perturbed.

The mountain calls me out of my tent,
Out to evaluate the route to take;
A technically easy one unfolds—but saddled with cornices in staggered
Rows, ready to crack and collapse at the slightest trek of my boots on top of
their swirled snows.

Dumb luck sometimes rules the day, and nothing might happen —
Except for my indelible remembrance of the fear that it might.
Remember the lure of the climb is the mountain's passive act of just being
"there" —
Daring you to trust to luck, to your own self-experience,
And to challenge us all to see what we can accomplish as members of the
human race.

Thus the saying goes: "nothing ventured, nothing gained,"
For it is rational to accept a calculated risk in relation to the significance of
the prize,
But know this well: the mountain can defeat the best-laid plans by a random
whoosh of its fickle winds.

For there is no one, no parent or other guardians to make things right again;
You're on your own now, free from all authority but that compelled by your own will's desire —
A *"Freedom of the Hills,"* as the textbook says, that entails acceptance of responsibility that you are equally prepared
To win, lose, or draw—a freedom to choose that can't ever be taken from you—except
By your own succumbing to a childlike faith and reliance on the kind assistance of others.

Border Peak

I glance upward toward the sky;

Your massive bulk shadows the valley,
Your summit ridge demarcates the boundary
Between one nation and another, which makes me wonder and ask just why?

As we prepare to ascend your snow-dome summit,
We tie up our gear till it snugly fits,
Like an astronaut going into space who never quits —
We resolve to reach your top without any fear to plummet.

As we step one foot in front and then the other
The summit ridge gradually emerges
And points the way to all our urges,
But though we slowly step, we begin to smother:

Your oxygen is too thin for our blood
The summit trail becomes obscured
'Til we have the nearly blind leading the nearly blind as though assured
That our way will not falter nor be rebutted.

The summit path begins to narrow
Until we dare not step further by choice
For fear that we might stand on an overhanging cornice.
Our vision now begins to clear as we begin to harrow

At the overwhelming sight unfolding at our feet that

Begins to give us vertigo to finish us off

Or spoil our vista and make us scoff

After all the energy, preparation, and skill, we must admit we're beaten.

But suddenly our focus returns

And all is laid out at our feet;

We need not fret about our deed,

Though we must never again fail to learn

The lesson that it's all a game of happenstance

Not worthy of a second chance.

Our descent generally retraces our upward trail

Until we spy a sickle-curved crevasse;

We deftly circumnavigate the hazardous, bottomless trench

That nature placed there to trap the vainglorious who believe they cannot fail.

And so we passed the last test well-prepared,

But most we knew was that we had never been scared.

Scene of the Avalanche

I lift my eyes to the hills
Where soaring spires seem to lunge toward the infinite,
Never to arrive there, always striving to scrape the heavens
In ironic representation of man's own vain attempt to rape the sky.

A swirling mist of white death envelops the precipices,
Plunging toward an unplanned destiny, smashing all who are enveloped
And dizzying those who stop and stare at nature's perfect balancing act:
This, the mountain's shedding its mantle of unbalanced snow
And causing havoc without a hint of feeling, without a tinge of remorse.

Where does the human form belong in this disjointed scene of amoral action?
Does the human have any place at all in this, nature's grand playroom without conscience,
Without judgment of right from wrong, without knowledge of good and evil, nor
Any consideration for the human's plight, nor any perception of the human's fright?
Nature's forum operates without any thought of the extent and consequence of its actions;
To this terrible truth, we must reconcile ourselves,
And not impute intent nor ascribe motive to nature's abstract conduct;

For, by definition, nature is a phenomenon unto itself, answerable to no authority;
Driven by its own volition, and free to strain at the infinitude of the sky,
Or to bury deep the human form beneath its uncaring, unfeeling torrent of massive
Crystalline bulk and insensate seracs that plunge and pierce us with their mass.

So why do I still have any thought that some silent, guiding hand still remains present —
If only to witness the wonder of its handiwork and the playing out of its predestined
Rules of fate on its glorious stage of Creation?

The Test

When preparing for an assault on a daunting North Wall, my
Guide first put me to the test in a *couloir*-gully of what seemed
Like nearly perpendicular ice and snow on a spur of a nearby ridge
That mimicked conditions I could expect to encounter on the North Wall itself.

I was beset by fear and trepidation lest my technique fail to impress
And pass muster, or, worse still, utterly and objectively fail to propel me
Upward with a rhythmic pace, but instead in the ungainly, awkward,
lurching motion
Of some unseasoned climber's uncoordinated flailings.

In the event, I surpassed my own expectations and smoothly, gracefully
ascended
In efficient sync with my lissome limbs—for a climber's "form" necessarily
"follows function" to the nth degree;

Jutting forward first the right arm and left leg, then the opposite, the left arm and
The right leg, with my brace of ice tool-swings, each being a solid sinker
planted firmly,
But not desperately—all in control of my fluid environment and my own
capability to adapt

To it in one seamless, even web of harmonious movement —
Till my form approached that of a vertical ballet on ice and snow,
Nearly (dare I say) attaining the suppleness of my personal paragon,
Catherine Destivelle, "*Le Danseuse De Roc*" or "The Rock Dancer" as
she is rightly termed—but here on ice and snow:

I was nearly 40, and truly on the top of my game, ready to take on the challenges I was expected to overcome while exhibiting the maturity of a Hemingway-Hero's grace under pressure.

My supposedly secret satisfaction at my performance, however, simply Oozed from every pore of my body—till the guide laconically said:

"Well, I've seen just about everything on this slope, and your technique is More than adequate for the trials to come."

A glowing, dark warmth of self-satisfaction surged through my body like Liquid fire as I gathered up in a coil my used-up rope behind me Always ascending ever further to the top.

I had finally achieved an assumed apotheosis of perfection that needs no advertisement:
Climbers value action over words in any event. And my action spoke for itself. The cobwebs of anxious fear dropped away from me like grime exposed to sunlight;
I had arrived, and all knew it—none could deny it. I had achieved far, far beyond that which I had dared to contemplate.

In the final event, the weather closed in on the North Wall of my aspiration And precluded all attempts for the duration of my visit: no matter—I had done What I had set out to achieve: garner the respect of my judges, who were now My colleagues and peers.

Second Thoughts on Conundrum Peak

You are nothing but a heaving, rolling lump of earth
Hurtling in frozen motion toward the sky;
What agonies did you exact until the
End of struggles toward your zenith came about,
But only after all those who had already died?

Must we suffer *in extremis* before we realize our earthly limits?
No one should perish in vain pursuit of hollow triumphs
That lack in thoughtful foresight.

Yet a craven bunch would we be if we sought
Safety for ourselves alone,
While watching others struggle mightily
Toward that alluring apogee,
While sneering at the sheer bathos —
An abrupt descent from the sublime to the ridiculous —
Of those who proudly conquer an utterly useless point
Merely hanging in the sky with nothing to justify its amoral ethos.

O frozen fortress that's free of care,
Why do you tug on me if not to snare?
So, after all, I, too, find myself drawn to storm
Your citadel of absolute abstract perfection,
Regardless of its obviously symbolic futility, or
Rather just because of it.

Encountering Mount Massive
(or sic transit gloria mundi)

Adrift amidst a sea of peaks, alone I ventured among the heights so bleak
That none did present itself able for me to seek a way to gain purchase
On a summit so sleek that mastery of it would be possible by even the most
meek.

What is my feeling in the presence of so daunting a massif that I tremble at
Its mere presence? Do I seek a way to avoid what seems inane grief,
Or do I merely stare at its form of no less than five points above 14,000 feet
in
Sheer disbelief?
I know that my time is finite and ultimately so brief
That I must consider ways to bypass its vast expanse and gain relief
From its oppressive bulk, and so defeat its natural blockade, not unlike a thief.

So why do some seek to ascend this mass precisely where there's the most
resistance,
And try their skills where there's the least hope of gaining assistance
From the natural contours of the land off in the distance, and proceed to force
Their will upon the slopes with grim persistence—contrary to nature's imposing
Lay of the land, and act out their own design with severe insistence
To the point of perversely risking their own existence?

Such a triumph of the will ironically compels the mountaineer to traverse
All five points before descent, or else risk failure to achieve a deed that
brings about a
State of being content, which the mountaineer ardently pursues without relent:

This drive is not merely a desire having a potent effect upon the climber's sense of time

Being well spent, but actually consists of a definitive event, that nonetheless passes silently without discernible moment —

For all worldly glory is fleeting.

Inclement Weather on Fair Mount Bierstadt

In mid-April we are used to expecting at worst
Blustery, unsettled conditions, but free of gale
So it was when we three awoke two hours before the dawn
Just to slip into our climbing, early-spring-weather clothing, and to pack
our gear.

Awake at 3:00 AM, departed at 4:00 A.M. from our snug den in Fairplay,
We reached the trailhead at 5:30 A.M. and tackled Guanella Pass;
We reached the summit via the northwest face more than 5-1/2 hours later,
ca.10:45 A.M. —
A surprising figure to be sure since it's only 2,500 feet over three miles to
the summit from the pass.

This should have told us that something was amiss on this tame mountain,
but we were distracted by daunting views of the imposing Sawtooth Ridge
connecting our Mountain and Mount Evans; the ridge still covered with ice
and snow, it was obviously no place to try to go.

So we began our down-climb, steadily at first, but then it became a frantic
race to the
Warm, still safety of our truck, as Mount Bierstadt then unleashed on us
everything it
Had, with hail, sleet, snow, and gale-force winds that blew a steady 30 mph
up to 40,
Gusts that knocked us just about off our feet. Nonetheless, we reached our
haven at
About 1:15 P.M.—in whiteout conditions.

We had blithely disregarded the fact that mountain ranges make their own weather

Systems, especially above 10,000 feet, where it can have frosty, steady gale-force winds,

While all below that height is fast asleep. Thus, full winter conditions prevailed in our scramble to the

Truck during ever-deteriorating weather, which made us feel very small indeed:

Helpless against the fickle weather that could have buried us deep.

Winter Ascent of Mt. Bross' "Windy Ridge"

Having the broadest summit of all the 54 Fourteeners, with just a small cairn marking its gentle prominence,

We had ascended by the South-East Ridge, called "Windy Ridge," of Mt. Bross, in full-on winter conditions in mid-February; we asked for no mercy, and expected none from this otherwise demure mountain in summer conditions. No matter, for all the mountains in the "Mosquito Range" are prone to stormy gales at all seasons, and only fools make the ascent unprepared for the worst.

Glissading down the North-East Ridge of Mt. Bross to the base of the spacious Cameron Amphitheater, and an old Jeep trail leading off the mountain's slopes altogether,

We had not had a grueling journey, except for those forever-moments suspended in time while exposed on Windy Ridge,

When we faced the ever-imminent "whoosh" that could have swept us off like specks of flotsam and jetsam to an ignoble oblivion of nameless caress at the base of the ravine, with our bodies to be found only in the spring thaw.

We reflected: just what had we added to our mass of experience in making this winter ascent?

Only the knowledge that the whims of the mountain spirits are painfully fickle and can let some pass wholly unmolested

While others are trapped in a tangle of unfortunate circumstances, one piled on another, coming on one by one, *seriatim*, each always giving the false impression that "the worst" is always "behind" the climber's travails.

So we were not certain of what great credit we could claim for a successful ascent of this normally tame mountain, albeit in mid-winter—for a successful ascent is always an anodyne against the empty feeling of struggle in vain futility—except for when it's not.

Escape from the Elements

With twilight fast approaching, we glissaded down the mountain's cramped, central *couloir*—an obvious avalanche chute—during the approaching dusk, calculating that the avalanche risk there was outweighed by the risk of not descending fast enough to outrun the swiftly approaching whirling blizzard that was menacingly closing in on the summit.

No time to linger and survey the domain we had conquered by our ascent— for the weather had turned tempestuous, with nothing but the shrill, driving winds of up to 40 mph and beyond—a real gale, and harbinger of a total "whiteout" yet to come.

So we consciously chose to risk the white death of an avalanche over the risk of being caught outdoors in a whiteout during the whirlwind of a snowstorm we anticipated was about to come. That's what our collective experience of exposure to the elements led us to decide: descent by any means was now immediately imperative.

We pulled out our ground insulating sheets, sat down on them, and propelled ourselves using our ice axes as paddles and as steering rudders as we slid down the narrow gully.

And what a wild slide of a ride it was! We all had to brake our slides with our ice axes to slow down the rate at which we were plummeting to the basin at the base of the mountain of our freely chosen fate.

In actuality, we secretly relished the sensation of beating the elements at their own game, becoming masters of our destiny, if only to be able to choose the least chancy risk of annihilation.

Failed Direttissima

On first catching sight of the splendor of the pristine "Rockwell,"
I stood awestruck in wonderment as it cast its spell
Upon me and my companions, who stood still in amazement
At the wondrous challenge it posed in the purity of its nascent,

Raw, untamed reaches of ridges and cliffs that, by this route, posed
An eternal dare to all those who sought to pierce its undisclosed
Privacy; we shuddered in anticipation of the struggle that just one fumble
Would exact in automatic consequence of one careless stumble.

Did we pause in trembling fear at the fateful outcome that could await
Our bold attempt at mastering its direct folds by this way, seeking to subjugate
Its heretofore unchallenged, random form that none had dared to dissipate
Into pieces that could be organized in conformity with the force of their will,
Making mockery of ages of aggregation of conglomerate upon that hill?

No, we had too blithely called the peak our own; a wiser and a chastened bunch we plunged
Our way downhill—never to call nature our own again lest we fall, lunged
Headlong to our demise: for the limits of our will had been tested.
And we found our strength had been sorely tried and wantonly rejected:

For nature respects no personal force of will, only natural laws that apply to one and all;
This, then, was to be our gift to humanity: not to succumb to that fatal flaw of *hubris* that
holds us all in thrall.

The Quest

The Freedom of the Hills

As is said in the first line of the first edition (1960) of the classic textbook "Mountaineering": *"The quest of the mountaineer, in simplest terms, is for the freedom of the hills..."*

Peering from my tiny ledge, I see the creatures below, carrying on like ants
While I am free of mundane worries and all the pedestrian "no, you can'ts."
Is this, then, the denouement of *"The Freedom of the Hills"?*
Examined carefully, at least three connotations emanate from this Motto's will:

First, there's the age-old adage, *"Montani Semper Liberi"* (*Mountain people are always free*),
A Latin slogan that surely rings true in the *Political* sense, for mountain people are bound only to their own ways, free from the constraints that others would impose on their days.

Mountaineers also enjoy freedom in the purely *Physical* sense, for they have chosen to
Cultivate technical skills enabling them to go wherever without any dread,
Even to places wholly frozen where others fear to tread...

But more subtly and importantly, mountaineers are also free internally in the *Psychological* sense, for they are more in touch with their aspirations in the "Pursuit of Happiness," as they conceive it than those who lack dedication to the heights, not even to try to achieve some deed of merit, and thus can only mock the mountaineer with supercilious disparagement born of ignorance or spite.

When in the heights, mountaineers are thus *free from the judgment of others* (except their peers who have already "been there and done that")—a wholly abstract freedom that in part
Carries on even while the mountaineer is on the ground.

Thus, an aspect of the "Rapture of the Heights" can be captured and carried to wherever
The mountaineer may choose to dwell in preparation for the next adventure, fraught
With doubt and fears of expectations.

This, then, is the quest that drives mountaineers wherever they may strive to embrace
A precious freedom that celebrates the mountaineers' own capacity to conceive of a test
Of their ability, and for knowing
Full well what others find only unduly inscrutable and daunting.

Glorious Failure?

Wounded, mangled, mashed and burst-asunder,
I rolled in squalor, awaiting my new challenger,
But I still retained the dignity of an unconquered,
Ravenous beast, though skulking for safety's sake,
But all puffed-up with the pride of the nobly defeated, still self-convicted of
the righteousness of the former, yet ineffable, clash.

They say the only causes to have proved they were worth fighting for are the
hopelessly lost ones that still retain all the fire and passion that had imbued
them with a certain special quality elevating their status to the fever pitch of
a searing blind faith *not comparable* with all those ordinary catalysts so-oft
invoked in the name of pursuing dangerous action.

The dusky campfire glow of dying embers that had once burned so hotly
Cannot belie the nature of the fiercely contested struggle, which had once
seemed
So consuming of all reality itself; where bodies, here and there, were strewn
about
In a seemingly senseless sacrifice.— be they dashed to death on the ridges
of rocks or lost somewhere in the maze of crevasses and caves.

Now all lay silent where they fell, but were too
Hazardous to extract from their precarious, contorted positions and unnatural
locations.
So their remains pose a danger to all who would dare venture to retrieve
them for
Conventional, devotional interment,

Yet the nature and quality of their demise testifies to the desperate efforts expended in their quest for enlightened transcendence in pursuit of the *"Freedom of the Hills"* — and far more nobly than any conventional tomb ever could.

Indeed, to let the Fallen lie where they fell is the greatest tribute that can possibly be paid to their quest for
the *"Freedom of the Hills"* — a freedom that mountaineers express in their exercise of the fundamental, government-protected liberty to what the Declaration of Independence calls the *individual's "unalienable" right to the "pursuit of happiness" [see p. iii, and p.116]* —
a right that mountaineering in its totality exemplifies o so well.

Second Thoughts Conceived in Trepidation

Alone I venture toward a fate unknown;
Filled with dread and regrets of my own.
Soloing is a transcendent step not to be taken with remorse,
But I can't help but feel that I'm undertaking a senseless *tour de force*.

Yet onward I endeavor to achieve my goal
With no compunction about damning my soul
To ooze freely with hubris visible to one and all,
Except there's no one here to witness my fall.

None but the mountain wall and I will know
The outcome of this, my spectacular gamble in the snow;
It's just for me and the vertical formation of rock and ice
To judge my skill and luck in this heartless game of dice.

So off I step across the yawning bergschrund, roped into my precarious ladder
Until I come face-to-face with the stupendous challenge that doesn't really
matter
To anyone who has his wits about him,
And knows my efforts can be erased in a moment by the mountain's passing
whim.

Yet I can't see the daunting odds, for I'm too close to my objective to form
a sound perspective.
I begin my ascent with wild abandon, free from the judgment of others and
their jealous invective.
But the mountain harbors no particular animus toward me:
It only sits in brooding wonder at all my struggles just to be free.
(And in the end, that's more than enough satisfaction even for me.)

Last Things

Last Gasp

Straining to cross the swiftly flowing current of the stream,
We roped up for safety's sake while scooting across a rotten,
Exposed log that had to serve as our trestle over the current below;
Then we climbed 2,700 punishingly steep feet, clinging to the mountain's
Northwest Face; the blueish, pre-dawn glow of the sun's aurora
revealed our precarious path, giving an eerie setting to the scene of
Pristine grandeur lying before us, which we were blithely content to sully,
No matter the majesty of the mountain's untrodden summit snows that
Silently beckoned us from above.

What had we come to seek at the mountain's lofty heights, so bleakly
Blocked by nature's design? I felt the oppressive weight of the mountain's
Mass bear down on me with every step taken up its daunting flank.
Yet, I continued undeterred, even spurred onward by the mountain's
Natural resistance to my hubris-soaked fleece, vainly intruding into the
Formidable fastness of the mountain's stronghold that remained elusive in
Its radically sloping summit's triangle.

No peace of mind, to be sure, nor solace in your recondite redoubt
Was to be found; just an inner, ineffable satisfaction that we were on
A trajectory that defied nature's boundary—but one that was sadly far
Beyond my ken.

Yet did I harbor a perverse glee at being precisely where nature
Commanded I ought not to be.

So, silently we still crept across an apparent path on your Northwest Face;
While everything was absolutely still, frozen hard in place.
Slowly, we sleeked through the tortuous trail that wasn't safe
Just so we could gain the final ridge leading cleanly to your
Summit's obscure zenith.

But we were finally, utterly blocked by a massive *gendarme* in
The route that, all agreed, just couldn't be "cinched"—*i.e.*, circumvented
Safely, given the weather conditions that had arisen,
The passage of time, and the limits of our
Technical prowess.

As I turned back, I dared to think of the summit—in a last gasp of
Noble futility, while proceeding toward the base of the mountain's
Imposing mass, with twilight fast approaching.

Coda

We strove along the exposed ledges,
Never to know the hazards that we tempted:
Each step was taken actually on shaky *terra infirma*
With childlike blind faith in our imagined bubble of security.

So we mustered all our strength to press on and on
So that we might encounter a vision of the summit, still veiled in mist
That obscured our vision of its transformative power,
Cloaked by its native hue of pale opacity shrouding in mystery
Our obscured perception of the ultimate reality
Lying somewhere, we felt, behind its façade.

We could hardly abide this aching delay in the consummation
Of our expectation of a revelation that drew us on like the Siren's call,
To meet ourselves up close in nature, to see ourselves naked, quaking
With our own desire to know each other's inner self, a reality that elsewhere
Paralyzes our inquisitive nature, for few want to know the *entire* truth
That comprises a human being's inner life: be it rapacious, tender, or just
bewildered.

When one realizes the vast forces arrayed against
Our knowing the "life of our mind": the resistances, the blockages
That we felt only the experience of gaining the summit could lay bare,
We still plodded along; but soon, we no longer wondered how we
compromise our ideals
And resigned ourselves to concluding that enough is enough —
All in exchange for some tawdry, transitory experience of spurious merit:

"Oh well, we didn't reach the summit this time,
But we gained so much knowledge reconnoitering,
Blah, blah, blah..." — till we convinced ourselves
That we achieved at least *some measure* of success,
Which in this case is worse than none at all.

To think that this tale of curtailed adventure
Could assuage my feelings of guilt in any respect,
That it would compromise my conviction to finish my tour would be merely puerile dissembling,
This, my time to overcome the mountain's features that jealously guard
Its *sanctum sanctorum* of essential truth.

And as we turned back, beset by the winds blowing horizontal sleet,
I know I trembled at the lost wonders that are revealed at the summit, and
The stab of piercing introspection induced only when reaching the summit —
All foregone despite the lure of its awesome grandeur.

Private Thoughts

Hopeless and Helpless

One day I awoke but remained still while I lay

Creaking, cracking, groaning and aching for all the rest of the day,

Till my strength poured out of me, and I was broken and humbled by the sheer mass of my own decay —

Crushed beneath my own burden of regrets that had always held sway

O'er my thoughts that consumed me with contemplation of the only way

That I could ever cleanse myself of my guilty deeds and cloak my failures, without dismay,

Or that I could ever free myself and yet not betray

My innermost thoughts of my failure to obey

My own restraints against self-slaughter that no force of will could ever belay:

How can I ever seek to allay

The depth of a pain that I can't convey?

(No matter the effort at straining to be fey, for

I can no longer struggle to project my spirit as once having been free.)

Time's Toll

Alone I ventured into the shadows of the cold,
Seeking that which would ultimately unfold,
Striving mightily against growing old;
Till time stood still while I never told
All those who would peer deep into my soul
Just how frantically I was pursuing my goal.
Only I knew the course of my next step
Would be to harness the ache that was scouring the depths
Of my fearful travails, and to struggle not to have slept away
My sole chance to stem the oozing increments of time that
Had persistently crept on and on, insidiously constricting the
Expanse of my quest not to let time dissolve my deeds of daring,
And to arrest that corrosive decay from mere time that had ended my
Best efforts to disguise the signs of times past;

As I grew older, time itself seemed faster and faster to pass:
Who will save me from my own decline?
Who can stop the passage of time?
"Seizing the day" only sharpens my sense that there's a line
Beyond which no one can alter the outcome fearfully seared into
My mind —
That all of life is a precarious existence that can be morally vacuous and
unkind;
But if I leave behind something of value contributing to the Life of our
Minds —
That then, when the end comes for me to recline, I can tenderly greet it,
Not totally purblind.

Then, and only then, can I smirk at time's cruel force that had made me
Quake with feverish trembling at the source of time's wanton ravages
Without remorse that mangles our magnificence, all in due course,
Without thought, without reflection, without any appreciation of its own
Malignant direction.

Masked Duplicity

I plod along from day to day
Wishing myself to be alone
In my time of trial and despair;
Not to spread my gloom around
And so poison the atmosphere
With my dismal thoughts,
When others should be light
And free from self-reproach —
Bathed in the pure glory of life,
Free to live their life just as it occurs —
While I dissemble one face to the
Judgmental world and
Deceitfully misprision another,
Deftly camouflaging that I'm but a
Cracked vessel that's no longer
Suitable to contain the exuberant vitality
Of youth.

Such is the fate of all old folk
Who outlive their function in its prime
And struggle to carry on in passing
Style their tasks with the usual aplomb,
Caught up in the appearance of the moment,
Always seeking to evade the time of judgment
When the truth seeps out, exposing their
Charade in a ceremony of shame and guilt
That reveals for all to see just how frail and fragile
We all prove to be, having outlived the time when
One could still contribute something of value.

A Meditation on Despair

When I ponder my innermost being,
Blank reality tells me that there's nothing to live for;
Nothing to strive for, nor to aspire to:
Trapped by past circumstance, I'm already damaged goods
Far beyond salvation, headed for damnation.

The knowledge of this condition saps the will
To persevere henceforth; what matter does it make
When I'm already scarred beyond my self-recognition of the man I once was:
Convicted of the past's burden beyond remedial action
So that any "effort" now builds on such rot and ruin as to
Render futile and cruelly ironic the goal of regenerating me.

It's said that the only causes worth fighting for are those that appear
To be the hopelessly lost ones; should I devote myself to salvaging a piece
of me?
And to what end?

Ah, for the sake of dignity in defeat, and defiance of my fate —
I will not let the worldly gods destroy me for their sport,
And will seek ennoblement by suffering out my destiny's string.
With endurance comes peace to my innermost being, my *neshuma*,
Which finds refuge in a confected self-worth crafted out of pretense,
posturing and dissembling;
Since the world judges by outward appearances, I must exhibit the

Proverbial "grace under pressure" in stoic fashion despite (and because of)
The wanton wreckage of my life.

Thus I persist, and desist from morbid, mawkish rumination;
And so carry on to the summit for honor's sake.

Persistence

Mutilated, invalidated, nullified, and smashed,
I nonetheless carry on for righteousness' sake;
Broken and crushed beneath a mass of outrageous affronts and countless indignities,
I humbly seek out a place for grace to enter and ennoble my life by placing
Trust in my faith that I was created for a worthy purpose, and retain basic dignity,
And that I do have something of intrinsic value left to impart, despite all events having militated against me;
So that I can still summon the will to struggle to explain myself to a
Quizzical world that judges by exterior checklists and leaves it at that.

I slowly saw a light that shone all day and night
And it was the light of the friction generated between good and evil,
Emitting sparks of energy that illuminated the void between them
And covered the gap existing between me and the rest of an indifferent humanity,
But which may from time to time have the courage and strength of will to observe
How the world was fashioned starkly without regard to right and wrong.

For at times I find myself loathing the world, and everything in it, including myself,
And can see no way before me except that of annihilation at the hands of my enemies, or myself, cruelly
Induced to act out of sheer despair at the hopelessness and futility of it all.
For I utterly revolt at the notion of taking so-called "responsibility" for my hopeless situation

When it was so unfairly imposed on me without my meaningful participation in my fate,
Such that all seems lost to injustice and hate, both of the world for me and me for it.

And I tire of explaining, and explaining myself to a puzzled and ignorant world
About how I was brutally knocked out of my rightful orbit, if I'm being truthful, or
How everything has worked out just fine, if I'm in a dissembling mood.

But the stars proceed in their courses without regard for my anguish, for I was helpless to battle the vast forces arrayed against me.
I am now but a lost life, *a life unlived,* a shadow of what might have been, constrained to live out a life of eternal failuredom, while I smile, and smile, and yet subsist in bottomless despair.

O where is there any relief from the oppressive reality of my present state of mind,
Or, rather, my actual state of being that would be in *anyone's* mind were he subjected to the savage degradation to which *I* was treated without relent, without pity to any extent.

Is there no hope of redemption, and enjoying peace of mind in this
Fallen and rushed world that has no time for the troubled of mind? I seek and find a salvation in my own thoughts and deeds, which the world cannot rip from me—unless I let it pollute my spirit any further, and thereby deny me my revenge of living out my time in a tranquil state of mind, as best as I can find it, and so experience an abiding peace with my past, liberated from dwelling with the perpetual contemplation of my woes and their all-too-familiar sorrows.

Broken Memories

Slowly, I stretched my contorted form
In between the shadows of an impending storm
Nowhere to be found among the living or the unborn
But slyly through the realm of the undead echoes
Of all those who had gone before; reverberating forever,
Unaffected by the living thoughts of those who dwell solely in the now.

The climber, though, senses the folds of time that
Linger o'er the present terrain that would present its appearance
As the only reality that ever was, insensate to the touch of
Those who were there before, and despite the lingering imprint
Of all those Seekers who had struggled and fallen where none would know
of their efforts or demise
Among the pinnacles and trenches of remote things gone by—far beyond
the reach of those who can sense what they see in only the here and now on
the shallow surface of
Present things that move along without regard for their missing past that
exists beyond the tick-tock of moving parts, which can nonetheless be
stilled in just a brief moment of passing time.

To climb where others have left their imprint, if "only" in the mind of those
who live in the moment,
Is to be part of the entire reality of a place, not just in one segment of its
existence, but for all eternity gone by: in communion with the past, present,
and things yet to come, "future" only in the sense of those who dwell locked
in their history, unable to search for their thoughts about the things that had
gone wayward, not able to seek out and feel the remnants of all that was lost
to time, nor what may yet come their way.

This faculty of apprehending the past and contemplating the future sets Humans apart from the animal kingdom, which exists solely in a "state of nature," aware only of the moment, and oblivious to the reality of once and future things to come. In this sense, Humans are immortal compared with other animals, for it is only we who can ponder our past and contemplate our future—all while existing in the present moment of real-time.

Cryptic Peak

Mountain, mountain, you are there,
Filling up the space and air;
Why don't you consume your share of creation's
Force and time, without a care?

Where do you exist in thought's phantom place —
Of wanton things that seek for grace,
Of abstract things that have no depth,
Of forgotten climbers who have lost their way,
Of those who seek to capture time's fleeting passage in a moment of
implacable will.

Or are you present only in the here and now,
Occupying a void without any idea about the reason how?
Just how long does your enigma plan to stay,
Or do you intend forever to tease and play?

But by your conquest the climber feels
As though he's triumphed over the ephemeral, and so he reveals
Your abiding presence that embodies those ideals
Of perfect symmetry that cannot otherwise be peeled
Away from your pristine form in which they're deeply sealed.

Yet there's nothing perfect in this world but the abstract thought
You inspire from your essence, which however has brought only
Doubt to all those who sought to master your mysteries
And who then became distracted and distraught.

So, now, where are those silent steps that trod this peak,

And strove to make it fall under the feet of yesterday's heroes

Who passed this way, never to be seen again, save in a moment of stubborn will,

To make palpable their inchoate triumph of their ageless struggle to

Reach beyond time's transitory moments, and make a mark that will endure:

No matter the commotion of all the crowds that come and go;

For it is only we climbers who stand and stare, yet still never know.

Sudden Insight

Imagine if you found yourself lying on a Creamsicle bed
With drenched tabs of paper full of insightful dread,
And there's no one to keep it cold until it melts;
Then all the seracs that hang over you fall onto your head;

It's then that you sense the folly of your endeavor as you slip
Into that second-self of sleep's fragile non-time:
Then you might intuit the presence of something else other than yourself
Running amok inside your mind.

How do you cope with the battle for your judgment and fulfill
Your duties, *e.g.,*
that to honor your parents, who
No longer experience life as you do in a single string of connected events,
But only in bits and parts, fits and starts, not as a continuous, integrated whole
Reflecting the values of your soul and your essence;

What if you drew back, dropped out, and let life take its course
Running roughshod over your conscience when all values, and your ego,
have collapsed
And become irrelevant, upside down, and inside out:

Only then, with this trans-valuation of beliefs, can you be free to extend
Your grasp to the infinite, and hold fast onto the certain, while discarding all
the rest; and recline serenely while the memories of the dead speak anew as
if alive; then you can behold a second chance to struggle with your destiny
unhampered by the "dead hand" of the past.

Warped Vision

I thought I had seen a guiding light
That shone upon me every night
With such intensity that it was always bright,
Until the day I saw its hidden source—despite
Its frantic efforts to keep me all affright;
Then nothing again ever seemed to be all pure and white.

For the light was that of bitterness burning contrite —
Nor did it give any fair hope that it might
Be an illuminating source that was intrinsically upright,
For it was poisoned with the equivocatory energy of fading twilight.

So what had led me astray like an unsuspecting acolyte,
And itself burned so hot it drove me into headlong flight
Was nothing but the Devil himself glowing in his own limelight,
And hailing for dupes who saw only what they wanted to think was right,
But who were seduced by the blinding sight
Of tainted purity that they thought had once fought the good fight, in spite
Of the odds against ever knowing right from wrong in this broken world of
pervasive blight.

In the end, who was left to judge me in my plight,
Where I had pursued an embittered course that proved only to sleight
The side that had seemed to set all things aright?
For the light had the power to ignite
A hatred that causes the hater to indict
Himself, and invites the hater to preclude all hope of ever experiencing any
future delight.

Free Will

I saw the light, and it was bright;
I saw the dark, and it was night.

The light did surround me all about;
But the dark did fill me up with doubt,

Which I chose to see was cloaked
With the pall of hate that choked

My every sense with inner rage,
Till better judgment entered the stage;

And left me naked in front of all —
Reduced to nothing but a cup of gall,

Which I did not drink for absolute fear
That it would rob me of all that I hold most dear.

And so I chose to carry on despite the hurt
Till I reached the top of my private turret,

Hiding high in the sky, far above my passing pain.

Epilogue: Time's Enigma

"*Where are the snows of yesteryear,*" asked the Renaissance French poet Francois Villon ("*Mais ou sont les neiges d'antan?*"), indicating the fleeting nature of our finite world (as I wrote on p. 31).

Indeed, our *actions and conditions* in this world seem transitory in relation to our being.
But a mountain itself seems permanent relative to ourselves, a fixture that may change in its appearance through the seasons, while its substance still remains fixed for an eternity of our time.

Though there may be no manifest evidence of past climbers' struggles on a route, the "absence of evidence" does not in itself indicate that there is an "evidence of absence"—for the lore of mountain tales forever echoes through the folds of time, passing from one generation to the next, *ad infinitum,* at least in our mortal perception of time.

There is also the perpetual Quest for "*The Freedom of the Hills*"—a freedom not just to be able to negotiate terrain that is denied to others because of the mountaineer's special training, equipment, and experience, but also *a freedom from the judgment of others* (except one's peers), *i.e.*, from the judgment of the general public, who can only look on in bewildered wonderment at the bold feats performed by the mountaineer acting in his special element (see pp. 112-13).

In any event, it is we ourselves who are transitory in relation to a mountain, which has experienced the comings and goings of generations of Seekers who leave little or no mark of their having passed the mountain's way.

Thus, the only record of our having existed, and of our bold achievements, would be that held in the *memory* of our collective progeny. This is what drives some men to try to "make *a name* for themselves," pressing the stamp of their personality onto the blank face of the mountain, and so *creating human meaning out of nothingness*—what I have previously termed the ultimate "existential act" (see p. 2)—for a famous deed will endure through the boundless reach of time.

While worldly "glory" itself may be a fleeting phenomenon (*sic transit gloria mundi*) (see p. 105-6), the very fact of the climb is a deed that cannot be erased from the memory of mankind—hence the phenomenon of mountain lore—which is the patina that coats our memories of past notable deeds that effectively live on forever—so long as the stories continue to be told.

Indeed, it is the very seemingly eternal presence of a mountain that drives a climber to assault its irksome fastness, and become the mountain's master, if only for a day. That achievement thus remains an enduring testament to the climber's sheer force of will, and that of his comrades.

Alan V. Goldman

Bonus Materials

Raucous Cure

People dissemble their silent sufferings;
Let us grow stronger by the sharing of them.
Silence is death by creeping inanition;
Let us not succumb to a lassitude born of world-weariness:

No, let the noise of our groaning wounds ferret out
The secret recesses of all silent suffering, and so liberate
Our pain—where it will cower before our collective shriek,
And shatter from the outpouring of our shrill cry that will
Excise the pain from its most reticent place of refuge: ourselves.

Vanishing Point

When I yearn for the unreachable, and cry for the broken of spirit,
My thoughts turn back to you—you seeming paragon of perfect proportion;
Unassailable, untouchable, you grip my very being, smirking at my
Insignificance; wryly do you tempt me, as I ache for your ever-receding
Horizon, just over there, but never palpable.

As my effort increases, so does my
Longing for your obscure zenith, always pulling me onward to my personal
Apogee, which is never quite enough to garner your laurels:
You are that point in the sky that vanishes as I reach it—a phantasm
That can never be grasped—only feverishly sought after, imagined,
And ultimately forsaken as an illusory aspect of infinity.

Intimate Conquest

As you prepare to tremble, shiver, quiver, and shake,
I dare to feel that I alone perceive that you shudder on the brink of eruption,
Retaining a dark, warm flood of liquid fire that is about to course through all the
Complex channels of your caldera—like pyroclastic lava about to flow freely
From a smoldering volcano, which is now emitting only noxious fumes.

Is all that pent-up energy that I sense truly yours or mine, or is it a mutual
anticipation?
Perhaps it is only that which is imagined in my distorted perception, con-
jured by a
Narcissistic and wishful imagination, skewed by a fanciful construction of
how things
Would have been in the primordial world, and may yet still be in the life of
the world to come?

My thoughts drew me toward the task at hand here:
On the winding volcanic rim, with slippery, steep, icy slopes
To the left of me, and smoking fumaroles emitting the foul odor
Of rotten eggs—sulfur dioxide—to the right of me, and having
A bottomless depth, I deftly stepped one foot ahead of another,
Moving unroped for the sake of others, since I knew that in this
Crumbling debris of rotten scree, no belay could ever hold; so
I gingerly moved along an unforgiving path, till I surmounted
Your rolling mounds of ancient decay, approaching the summit
Flag in disbelief at having overcome all your intricate blockades
And snares, and despite my display of overt apprehension, I had nonethe-
less retained my innate composure—for all the while I knew that I had
never been afraid.

Terra Incognita

A silence that is shattered by the shifting of frozen blocks of ice grating
Against one another;
Unseen, but lurking deep beneath the surface of what seems tranquil and serene:
Not unlike the subtle realignment of long-held beliefs that had, over time,
Seemingly composed the construct of one's outward character, and *persona*, but were
Actually dislodging the pillars of faith that had held one's belief system
Interlocked in place.

This slow-motion corrosion of self-convicted articles of accepted truth creeps
Crackling along, eroding the concept of faith; this dissolution of values leaves
One stripped of confidence in the outward appearance of nature as being the
Hallmark of reality, and foists upon one the moral obligation to establish one's
Own, self-defined values and truths in a world bereft of received wisdom.

Humanity is thus challenged to forge its own destiny by its own hand—a
Definition of the boundless freedom posed by the constant uncertainty
Created by the self-constructed, progressively unfolding architecture of an
Inescapable existentialist reality.

The figure of the mountaineer must, therefore, ultimately "believe" only in himself, and
Knows that the perceived world may not be what it seems, cannot be trusted, and that
Even the most intimate human relationships are subject to the whims of
force majeure

Yet while in this uncharted ground, one is nonetheless obliged to forge a
New moral compass, but one that is still cognizant of the eternal truths of
knowing right from wrong,
And capable of appreciating the nature and consequences of one's actions.

So when tragedy strikes, one must carry on as a cohesive unit for the good
of all,
Dedicated to the mission at hand, and engage in private mourning only on
One's own time, at a later date. In this way, we can indeed see further than
Those engulfed in their own woes, for we have benefited from the travails
And wisdom of all who came before us,
As Isaac Newton and many others have said, and have seen further only because
We have stood on the shoulders of giants.

Alan V. Goldman

Fear and Flow

Just a pitch further, just a bit more of resolve over fear;
Would I last the final stretch, or succumb to acrophobia and bail out
Just below the finish?

I imagined myself in a world apart from where I was, so as to remove my mind
From where I actually was, and
I became wholly self-contained and isolated from the surroundings about me:
I felt insulated as if in an imagined womb of security,

And as my vision narrowed to focus further on the task at hand,
I lost situational awareness of the *mise-en-scene* everywhere about me
And my world became ever smaller, focused on the
Activity I was performing at the time and perceiving nothing else.

Thus, my actions and awareness merged into a holistic endeavor;
I even thought I saw myself in the process of doing my own task;
Truly, I was in a concentrated state of flow, blocking anything that would impede
My performance of one small, successful job after another, and then another,
Always self-reenforcing my incremental, successful achievements
In a rhythmic, almost monotonous manner, robotic-like—uninterrupted by the
Daunting and fearful distractions of the outside world and my actual condition
within it:

For by now I was the master of *my* world and everything inside *it*:
I pledged to myself "never to look down" and risk vertigo, but instead
To look directly into the rock-wall, at my hands, where the scale of my effort was
Controllable and recognizable, of human-sized dimension.

My humanity accordingly prevailed over the inhuman challenge and proportion
Of the vertical slab of nearly sheer granite that loomed before the summit trail.

Lost Time

Every single moment in time lasts forever in the parade of events
Outside its own context, then reappears as a starkly isolated memory
That emerges only in the fabric of our dreams, transcending
The bounds of time and space, fresh as though it had occurred
In the here and now, but then eerily recedes, fading from our recollection,
Dissolving its own permanence—only to be resurrected in a flash night-
time vision
Of how things had once been: for the dead never really perish as
They persist in the telling of tales of ancient times gone by.

So how can we recapture the transient reality of recollections about
Our lost friends, and that of our own lost time?

Where are the signs of times past?
Where are the memories of past times stored?
Where is the security of past times stored?
Where is the security of lost innocence buried
If not in the fond remembrance of our experiences
As though no time whatsoever had elapsed since the events?

Ah, they persist in the communal celebration of our perpetual hope in
The future of things yet to come that will *enhance* the meaning
Of our past experiences, and reveal their ultimate significance.

New Content

Introduction

This separate collection of fifty-five poems explores the interior life of the mind as it reacts to a variety of themes and situations arising most distinctly in the austere arena of the high mountains. Unlike the poems in the prior section of this book, these are not primarily drawn from *my* special mountaineering experiences (although a few certainly are), but rather reflect on universal themes and situations that are especially prominent in the mountain environment. Collectively, these poems constitute a "meditation" on the nature of reality itself as perceived in the context of exploring the limits of human understanding and achievement.

The poems are loosely grouped under five headings, or chapter titles, but sometimes contain concepts that traverse constricting categorizations. Indeed, the poems reflect the reality of my belief that such human thoughts cannot be corralled and still retain all their intended meanings. Moreover, I feel that language constructed to convey but one thought does not reflect the manner in which human deliberation actually functions. Of course, language can convey one prevailing concept—but in the absence of any collateral ideas, the expressed thought falls flat.

(1)

In any event, the collection's first heading, *Confronting the Mountain's Challenge,* contains poems that reflect the varied situations in which climbers deal with the perpetual challenge posed by the very fact of the mountain's existence. Such situations may give rise to contemplation of the most abstract notions of perceived reality, and in doubts about whether the mountain is even "worthy" of our efforts, especially if attainment of the objective, obviously the mountain's summit, is too fraught with danger as to spoil appreciation of the potential rewards for success. Also, enjoyment of the challenge itself can be tarnished and consumed by the petty consequences of a climber's failure merely to have *properly prepared* for the task at hand, *i.e.,* to have correctly anticipated all the difficulties that will be encountered in the journey to the summit.

Further, the traditional challenge posed by a mountain, *e.g.,* deprivation of creature comforts and a sense of futility in striving for the summit, is reflective of a spirit of adventure that cuts across many fields of endeavor, including coping with the risks encountered in military operations, as well as self-doubt about the value of the sought-after goal or destination. Enjoyment of the splendor of the *"great outdoors"* and its natural energy can easily be dissipated by the inordinate, almost inhuman *effort* required to participate adequately in an alien environment, with all its unforeseen complexities and demands.

(2)

The second heading, *Time's Passage in the Mountains*, contains poems addressing the climber's sometimes distorted perception of time's passage in the disorienting and exotic surroundings characteristically found in the high mountains. For instance, there is the so-called *"buzzing of the bees"* (the kind of sound made by the discharge of static electricity stored in clouds that come into friction with each other and the peaks) and other sounds and events unique to the mountain environment (such as the subterranean creaking and cracking of snow slabs)—all of which seem to be occurring in *"real-time"*. By contrast, the climber hangs suspended in his ropes, feeling artificially detached from the strange natural phenomena all around him and other circumstances over which he has no control, but can only observe—which all contribute to a climber's feeling that, for him, time has effectively *"slowed down"* inside his gear-bound bubble, relative to the mountain's ongoing display of natural phenomena unique to the obscure, rarefied environment found only in the high mountains and mountain ranges.

(3)

The third heading, *Insight and Situational Awareness*, deals with the climber's struggle to attain self-knowledge through his encounter with the mountain's presence and nature—one point being that the mountain is, indeed, "there," as the saying goes. This truism actually becomes significant when the climber realizes that, despite the mountain's self-evident presence, it cannot engage in a search for self-knowledge and examine the *content* of its existence, wholly unlike the climber, who is enjoined by Socratic philosophical principles to recognize that the highest duty in life is to *"know thyself"* and to recognize that *an "unexamined life is not worth living"*. Given these injunctions, a climber may apply his knowledge about himself in dialectical opposition to the conspicuously *non*-"self-aware" nature of a mountain. In this regard, a primary purpose of the climber is to become ever-*more* "self-aware," thus wholly unlike the inanimate mountain, which does indeed remain in perpetual *existence*, but only in a purblind manner.

Furthermore, the mountain's existence is static—again, wholly unlike that of a human being, and particularly of a climber, who has the ability to engage in perpetual expansion of his self-knowledge by resorting to *existentialist* principles that posit a person is nothing but what he makes of himself, thus possessing a god-like "creative" power; indeed, *unbounded* creative power.

Also critical to realize is that a mountain's nature, quality, and features exist, at least in relation to humanity, only in the *eye of the [human] beholder* and are thus, like a work of art, wholly subjective.

(4)

The fourth heading, *Force of the Mountain's Presence*, contains poems illustrating the kinds of activities and events that often occur in the mountain arena, including avalanches (and avalanches of thoughts in the mind, see poem #23 "*Wild Structure*"), as well as poems addressing circumstances involving the climber's having to cope with the presence of a mountain and the kinds of emotions that the mountain evokes. Also addressed is the climber's attitude and impressions toward the mountain's form, and the complex feelings that the mountain *inspires* in the climber.

One poem, #29 "*Perpetual Challenge,*" is a good example of a cross-thematic poem of the sort I discussed in the second paragraph of the *Introduction*, above. I categorized "*Perpetual Challenge*" as a poem belonging under this heading, and not the first (*Confronting the Mountain's Challenge*) because I viewed it as describing the *effect* of the mountain on the climber far more than the *climber's* effect on the mountain, but there's room for debate.

(5)

Similarly, in the fifth heading, *Evaluating the Moments of a Mountain's Reality*, there is poem #34, "*The Power of Attraction,*" which on the surface could instead be placed under the fourth heading, above, *Force of the Mountain's Presence*. Yet I viewed poem #34 as primarily describing the unique nature and quality of the mountain's "come-hither" call (*i.e.*, the reality of the mountain's power lay in sometimes having a quasi-sexual quality), more than dwelling upon the stark fact of the mountain's "force" as such. Again, there's room for debate, but the poem illustrates how difficult it can be to categorize a work of art.

The poems under this fifth heading fundamentally concern the attractive qualities of the mountain; *i.e.,* quite literally, the moment when the climber senses aspects of the mountain that exert both a strain upon his will, virtually daring him or her to attempt to surmount the peak, and the dangling of an elusive "reward" for attaining the destination (see a poem already listed under a prior heading, #18 *"My Self-Struggle"*—again illustrating how the poems can build on each other and interrelate). This is a situation in which the climber envisions what new world would emerge after the drive to reach the summit is finally satiated.

The distinction from poems under the heading *"Confronting the Mountain's Challenge"* is that the poems under this heading deal more with the internal, psychological drive to understand the various meanings of the mountain's attraction, or the nature of its reality, rather than prior poems addressing feelings that emerge after having surmounted the summit (such as poem #22, *"Striving for the Top"*), and which seek to understand the essence of that reward (see poem #24, *"Renewal"*).

(6)

In this section, called "Afterthoughts," I reflect on some incidents and circumstances not fully set forth previously and seek to present poems that distill the essence of the core themes that animate my Book. (see poem #55, *"Expression of the Will"*). In those poems I seek to present a cogent summary of my philosophy about the meaning of mountaineering.

Conclusion

In any event, for the purposes of this *Introduction*, it is enough to say that while there are distinctive qualities to each poem listed under its particular Heading, in some ways, the new poems in this part of the book possess a variety of interrelated concepts interlocked by experience. Thus, the poems viewed as a whole represent a unitary philosophical *Gestalt* more than an interpretation of a specific event that in some fashion merely shares certain underlying principles.

This was the case with the relatively specific circumstances explored in the prior eighty poems in this Book. In an important way, the new poems well-illustrate the holistic nature of the climbing experience and that, while handily convenient, one cannot simply surgically slice the experience into separate segments. That is so because everything, every event that occurs in the sport of mountaineering, is infused with some elements of the entire body of experience and learning accrued over a considerable period of time—at least over the past one hundred or more years since the sport's inception during the mid-Victorian age, which is widely recognized as having given birth to the concept of "mountaineering" as we recognize it today.

Table of Contents

Force of the Mountain's Presence

Evaluating the Moments of a Mountain's Reality

Afterthoughts

Confronting the Mountain's Challenge

1. Confronting the Mountain's Challenge

Clinging to you for fear of falling into a bottomless void,
I clutched my ice axe 'til my fingers grew numb with cold
Pressure—as cold as the axe's cold-conducting shaft itself,
So that without my Dachstein, pre-shrunk, woolen over-mitts,
My fingers would have surely frozen solid to the frigid shaft's
Ambient temperature, stuck as if affixed with superglue—
Not to be freed without shearing away my fingers' skin and
Surface flesh in strips of freeze-dried, congealed clumps
Of blackened, bloodless, lifeless, wasted human dross.

Just what environment had I trespassed into to be trapped in
Such fateful circumstances? Had I blithely overstepped some
Interdict between one world and another not meant for human
Habitation?

If so, just *why* had I sought out a forbidden world, lost to humanity's
View without any loss of our capacity to thrive in its absence?

Well, it would seem that the human spirit compels us to seek challenge,
Indeed, veiled challenge, wherein we cannot even perceive the nature and
Quality of the risk that the adventure may pose—or else we do wither,
Wilt, wane and fade into an oblivion of our own making; rather, we would
Seek out confrontation with an oblivion beyond our restricted,
Circumscribed horizon, posing the eternal question ennobling the Human
Condition: *What's over there? What's on the other side of that hill?*

We must know.

I submit that it is *this* characteristic that distinguishes us most sharply from
The rest of the "animal kingdom"—for, other than the domestic cat, to
Which we impute our own "curiosity"—an animal is ordinarily content to
Dwell where it finds itself, unless prompted to move in a necessary search
For food—but *not* driven by an abstract, inquisitive wonderment about
What may lie ahead.

2. *Alone*

Alone I spied your paths to nowhere;
And strived to follow some path on your
Slopes that leads to somewhere, lest I realize
That my quest for your only heir – an incorporeal
Pristine shining city in the air – was fated to
Fail, when I awoke from the trance you had cast
That had led me to abandon all respect for due care
In feverish pursuit of the aspirations that always ensnare
The hopeful visions of youth without regard to having
Been captured in a moment of being cruelly mislead
By devices of their own unknowingly reckless despair.

And alone it is that I persist in a vacuum created by your
Sucking up all the atmosphere surrounding your bulk,
Your "Immunity zone" – of no escape – for like an "event horizon"
Bars even light from escaping from a Black Hole, your very presence
And power of attraction overwhelms my desire to freely forge my
Own path, independent of your paths to nowhere smothering
My ambition to make a mark of my own, leading outwards from
Your seemingly intractable sphere of influence:

And so I continue to strive all by myself – alone – to erupt from your
Zone of control, even over my own desire and longings, which hold
Me back from achieving some independent deed of renown, known
By all to be uninfluenced by your continuing gravitational-like pull on
My will to scale your vertiginous, irregular heights.

3. On First Apprehending
the Vision of a Mountain

Magnificent illusion before me, what is the key to understanding the
Nature of your reality? Does it lie in perceiving that you consist of nothing
But rock, snow, and ice? Or does it lie in recognizing that your
Amalgamation over the eons of time represents a force of nature, a spirit
Full of spice? What do my senses tell me is actually yours, and what is
Conceived of only in my mind?

Suddenly, an inner voice speaks to me and reveals that you are that which
You may become in my thoughts — indeed, a mundane challenge, a
Physical hazard, but one that's nonetheless besotted with my dreams.

Ah, my dreams of what you represent to me are immutable, regardless of
My tenuous position on your slopes.

Indeed, they are that much heightened when I encounter my most dire
Circumstances, for these only provoke further speculation as to the actual
Conditions prevailing at your summit, though they be cloaked in
Mysterium tremendum.

What force of nature or man could possibly reveal your inner sanctum for
All to gaze upon its hidden folds, leaving nothing but wonder at its secret
Places where one fears to tread, as if violating some primordial ban on
Uncovering your inner being, your inner meaning, your animate soul.

Nothing comes of nothing, or so we're told, but if that's true, how and Where did the first *perceived* "nothing" come into being? One must Perceive the evidence of absence, and this requires *a perceiver* with the Knowledge of distinguishing nothing from something — whatever form it Takes — and that knowledge precludes the existence of nothing as the Primordial state of being.

Ah, mountain of my vision, do not ensnare me in your riddles of causality; I would have been content just to have surmounted your summit.

4. Vain Exertion

Straining, striving, pressing onward 'till I can't take in another breath,
Ever falling behind my guide whose lanky stride exceeded my own, so
That his footprints in the virgin snow-pack didn't aid my following steps.
Thus, I resigned myself to abject failure, subject to ridicule and annoyance
By the other members of our party — for I was the first and not the last in
Line behind the guide, thereby impeding the progress of the other climbers
Along the practice plane, as they anxiously awaited my vain attempts to
Sink into the footprints left behind by our guide, who was "breaking in
The trail" on behalf of us all. Too timorous at first to ask the guide to
Shorten the length of his stride for my convenience, I struggled mightily to
Fit into his shoe imprints, while I became ever-more stressed by both
Physical exhaustion and mental anxiety about the outcome of our
Endeavor.

How was I to extricate myself delicately from the awkward predicament
Into which I had ignorantly and foolishly fallen? (I had known full well
That the guide was about 5 inches taller than I was, and that his normal
Stride would naturally reflect that.)

The answer is that no subterfuge will suffice, and I just had to summon the
Courage to request the guide to shorten his stride, even though I feared
(Without cause as it transpired) that this might mean his assessment of my
Capabilities would likewise be diminished.

In extreme sports, and in climbing especially, there's no slick substitute for
Revealing the Truth, which will out itself given the appropriate
Circumstances. When the environment thrusts one to the point of being *in*

Extremis, the acid test of deciding whether to confess the truth will *always*
Be the only rational "option" — for dire circumstances peel away all
Pretense, and strip one of all attempts at prevarication.

Not to acknowledge one's true situation necessarily leads to disaster,
Whereas honestly confronting the situation at hand at least holds forth the
Potential of salvation. My experience has taught me that there's simply no
Room for unjustified vanity — *i.e.*, foolish "vainglory": in the elements, a
Climber's "will"— however steely — hardly ever triumphs alone.

Alan V. Goldman

5. Elegy For The Fallen

Who mourns for those who perish on such summits as "The Deadly Bells"
(Maroon and North Maroon Peaks)? Are not those casualties to blame for
Their own misadventures? Why should society care about those who
Gambled and lost in an infamous game of chance, usually not thought to
Be worth a second thought?

O, because we are all engaged in a holistic endeavor, in which the
Mountaineer merely represents the "tip of the spear" of all humanity's
Quest to prevail over his environment; so that there is actually no
Dichotomy between "them" and "us," *i.e.*, the mountaineer, and the public.
For the mountaineer is but a proxy for the mass of mankind. As always,
Those who can do, do; while those who cannot, watch in awe and wonder
At the daunting feats performed in the name of humanity.

Thus an unspoken bond is forged between the active and the passive –
Never to be severed by the perception of different roles played by the
Whole band of those who share in a collective striving for the limits of
Human achievement.

6. Nocturnal Ascent

Clinging to the edge of tomorrow that we never wanted to come
For fear that it would bring yet another shower of unstable scree and
Shards that had been frozen in place overnight, we humbly cowered as
The dawn emerged from the edge of the nighttime's terminator,
Gripped for the expected onslaught of sedimentary fractile rock and
Expecting the seemingly set ones to fail once again in the very moment of
Reliance; for we had been night-climbing by headlamp and moonlight
As it refracted over the consolidating firm and thin layer of onion-skinned
Ice that mercifully glistened to illuminate our path, but would be gone in
The light of day, together with any semblance of stability and security that
We had gratuitously found prevailing at night.

Was our continued ascent during the clarity of sunlight worth the risk of
Random bombardment by sedimentary shards and failing rock features
That crumbled all of a sudden just while being relied upon? No; it was
Best to entrench as possible by day and move only by night.

The mountain was a deathtrap that lured the overeager tyro to his fate; we
Planned on meeting our destiny with eyes wide open during the frigid
Night, for no matter how crippling the cold might seem, it provided a
Route that was negotiable and suitably reliable, free from the incessant
Hail of the crumbling ancient seabed that had been upthrust by receding
Water levels, and which now posed a natural hazard to anyone who dared
To traverse its surface.

We summited just before dawn, and planned to wait out the day in the thin
Air of the windy peak rather than chancing descent on the fickle and
Fearsome rock during the daylight; but by our choice and serendipitous
Ingenuity, we had prevailed against nature's rawest, insensate elements.

7. Mountain of Our Dreams

The mountains are always with us and *in* us,
As the naturalist John Muir observed when first in
The Sierra. *I* feel their tug at our bodies and teasing of our minds,
'Till we react by striving to vanquish their summit,
Or yield to the allure of an ethereal abstraction,
And a notion of perfection, that their summit typifies
All so well.

What archetype of spiritual purity embodies
The concept that the summit represents to us
Something more than just a mound of dirt?
The answer lies in the inner reality that the
Mountain we are truly climbing is the one
Lodged deep within our minds... We confront
Ourselves — our hopes, ambitions, fears and
Doubts when we engage in the outward process
Of climbing the physical mound of earth before us.

Psychologically, we accomplish a *transfer of affect* —
Our state of mind being imputed *to* the mountain —
By actually climbing the mountain of our dreams, and
Not the heap of earth astride us.

That is the notion of abstract perfection which we pursue
With such seemingly desperate, ardent abandon;
Therein lies the motivation that spurs us on to astonishing
Feats of endurance and parlous acts of technical wonder.

This is the process that transports us into a state of ecstasy,
Almost literally: for we are lifted out of the shell of our bodies
And transported to the diaphanous realm that envelopes our minds.

Alan V. Goldman

8. *True Glory*

Encroaching upon the stuff of legend, I dared to doubt the value of
Radically audacious feats (such as free solo) performed by those who
Came after me, and who had laid claim to
Achievements that surpassed my ken, even
Passing beyond the comprehension of the
Range of my imagination — so startling was
The nature of those feats in their breadth and scope of
Accomplishment that I lay dumbstruck in awe
At the audacity of those persons who undertook
Such a challenge to attain their outlandish goals
That simultaneously approached the near-infinitude of abstract perfection.

Who could even endeavor to achieve such an aspiration?
Not I, for I was such a novice Seeker after the embodiment of
Such flawless deeds that I wilted at the prospect of ever following in the
Path of those dauntless persons who had attained the far-fetched
Object of their self-imposed designs:

For I had always felt that the mysterious glory and nobility of climbing, as
In *any* self-expressive art form, lay in the *quality of the artist's struggle*,
Which can best be experienced in the *im*perfect, so long as the goal was
Worthy, and not, necessarily, in the reaching, *vel non,* of any perfect
Finish line.

As the poet Robert Browning said: *"Ah, but a man's **reach** should exceed
His **grasp**, or what's a heaven for?"* (*Andrea del Sarto,* lines 97-98)
(Emphases added). How aptly this applies to rock-wall climbing!

In any event, the unique story of humanity, which sets it apart from the Rest of the "animal kingdom," lies in its *struggle* to achieve self-Improvement — certainly not in its actually having *done* so, even Assuming, *arguendo*, that such improvement is attainable, or desirable.

9. On The Nature of Challenge

Breathlessly approaching the limits of human endurance,
We warily approached the overhanging rock-wall, where
Our existence would hang upon not our own strength, but on
The physical integrity of the granitic slab to which our ironmongery
Would be attached, and to the strength of that gear itself, as well as
Our own skill in its proper placement.

We do not stop to ponder whether something is a worthy goal
Simply because, no matter the extent of its challenge, we can overcome it.
No, the challenge spurs us onward simply "because it's there,"
As Mallory's saying goes; indeed, are some humans innately predisposed
To accept such a challenge — is the drive integral with their human spirit?

If so, is the rest of humanity deficient in its aspirations, or merely not in a
Position to engage in such adventures, however misbegotten or
Ill-conceived, but who *would* take up the challenge if presented with
Enabling circumstances and tempted by peers?

O, the urge to sustain risk for reward, however abstract, *is* most likely
Intrinsic to the human condition, for our species has always sought out
New lands, new goods, and new opportunities, both for communal growth
And self-aggrandizement.

Today, in the *absence* (for some) of any further material need for food,
Shelter, and other sustenance, how does this drive to seek new challenges
Manifest itself? For some souls, it lies in striving to achieve further
Self-imposed goals, even if (or maybe because) those goals entail
Personal risk.

Indeed, Lionel Terray famously wrote a book about achieving the
Seemingly pointless, namely, *"Conquistadors of the Useless,"* which I feel
Frankly bares the aspiration to attain some achievement, and through that,
A sense of self-fulfillment, in the modern, mundane world.

This unquenchable spirit to conquer has wide applications in all fields of
Human endeavor, naturally including the military, for as the British *SAS*
Motto (sometimes Attributed to its founder, Sir David Stirling), goes:
"Who Dares Wins".

So the impulse to sustain risk for some perceived reward is indeed
Essential to fulfilling the human spirit; it is not to be made mock of by
Those who are not Seekers.

In our own adventure, the increasingly steep incline of the slope had
Finally reached my personal limit of enjoyable risk — when the cliff
began
To have a negative (overhanging) incline — and so I left those pitches to
The highly technical climbers who were qualified to cope with such a
Feature.

After all, one cannot experience the exaltation of achievement — even if
The goal is attained — if one had to experience naked terror, instead of
Enjoying a sensation of positive "flow," or was able to channel the risk
Into a negatively animated flow, as I wrote in my poem *"**Fear and Flow**"*
(See p. 153.)

10. Lost Redemption

To stop and see the splendor that does touch
The edges of the sky and so absorb the grand
Vista that envelopes our senses is an idle,
Though brief, diversion we can ill-afford while making
Our ascent, and yet is the *raison d'etre* that does
Forever animate our souls.

And so we sweat along the taxing route
That slowly drains our steadfast will to crest
The now-emerging summit, almost always
Cloaked in its grey mist and shroud, not unlike like
The scales that would obscure our vision of your peak
In Perpetuum — were it not for some
Strange mystic ray of light emanating from the
Twilight glow of your occult mountain *massif* —
To which we were so sedulously drawn
To seek out in the first instance, hoping to find
Insight into our very being.

Our journey ironically failed to reach its destination:
Although guided by the energy of the mountain,
We ultimately became exhausted and lost our way.

Time's Passage in the Mountains

11. *Parlous Tomorrow*

Clutching at the strands of yesterday,
I slid into the inevitable reality of
Things to come, but without embracing
The fullness of tomorrow in all its novel
Happenings yet to fill and burden my
Restless soul with the foreboding knowledge
Of whatever unfolding developments it may hold:
My ordained fate, my sealed destiny.

O where is the lodestar or mountain massif that will
Anchor our drift towards the unknown?
Is there no cynosure that will attract
Our attention onto the immutable
Values of yesterday —

Luminous values rooted in the past
Even as we hurtle headlong into the
Tenebrious world of tomorrow?

Whither are we tending, rushing forward into
An opaque universe that may hold murky
Happenings rather than radiating hope?

Hope for the future is no excuse for
Abandoning the established virtues
Of the past; truly, time has taught us
That not everything that is
"New" is necessarily "improved," and that
Not everything that is old is necessarily obsolete.

12. The Melody of the Mountains

Suspended by our swaying ropes, we perceived
That, for us, time had silently slowed down
Relative to the perturbed happenings occurring all about us:

The driving sleet, then the crackling mountain mist, also known as the
"*Buzzing of the bees*," as the rarefied air filled with static electricity
Signaling us to swiftly shed our ice axes and go to ground;

The groaning moans of misaligned slabs crunching together in the
Creaking snow-pack;

And the whining shrieks of pelting rocks-shards bombarding the earth
Beneath our feet —

All occurring in "real-time," even as we heard this mixed cacophony
drone
On and on while we hung dumbfounded in mid-air, feeling like intrusive
Observers of this naked display of otherwise occult natural phenomena.

Were we no more than passive partakers of this symphony of the
Mountain's melodies, or were we actually a holistic part of the grand
Design of the world's marvels, splendid in their showcase of which we
Were a separate, but not alien, presence after all?

We dared not answer this presumptuous question, for we were but puny
Creatures cringing in the veiled hall of the mountain spirits themselves.

13. Fated Condition

O Mountain, looming ever so close,
Did the forces that made you ever
Begin to realize how you would so engross
Those who dwell under your spell that they
Would be compelled to undertake truly grandiose
Schemes just to bring you down closer to us?

Or otherwise propel us to ascend your heights,
Not knowing our fate, toward your summit
Or be drawn ineluctably to reach for the sky that you seem to inhabit —
This, despite the danger of their risking a headlong plummet?

I dare think *not:* for to do so would be to presume
Upon the Creation's Grand Design in whose womb
We all were fashioned, and to doubt the Creator's plan
For how our fate is to be reprieved or doomed.

O Mountain edifice, are you actually part of me,
Or are you a self-contained entity that's free
Of me — of the key to my understanding my place
In the overall system of grace that ennobles my
Otherwise vacant, inane striving for your
Summit's resplendent place in the veiled design
Found in your recondite space.

14. Into the Realm of the Mountain Gods

Insolent, you self-exculpate yourself by having to furnish no *alibi,*
For you are **always** "there" — a presence looming above underlings
Who scrape at the sky when they brazenly dare to seek your summit;

Little do they know that they are entering a different realm of being or
Reality where one's mind is captured by dwelling in the space of abstract
Ideas: The very *concept* of a summit corrupts the life of their mind by not
Having given fair warning that they are trespassing into the plane of
Perfection,

Of archetypal representations of a perfection that doesn't exist on earth,
And are not meant to be comprehended by mortals whose very presence
Was not foreseen in this wilderness devoid of sentient beings, nor
Welcome in this parnassus of poetic composition.

Disappointment at failure to gain the summit is so easily transposed into
Self-castigation for "failure" to achieve mundane goals that are so trivial
In the grand scheme of things that climbing should not be undertaken with
Any expectation of success; indeed, it is the very *uncertainty of the*
Outcome that is the draw of adventure, which must necessarily unfold in
Its own fashion.

And the concept of ideal perfection in the mountain realm
Existing only outside the mind still remains pristine.

15. *Journey to the Extremity of the Mundane*

On May 15, 1997, as the climbing log will show,
Louis W, Dawson II, David Eye, and I myself
Deigned to make the by-now *de rigueur* slog
Up from Halfmoon Creek to the summit of bland
Mount Elbert, at 14,433 feet, Colorado's undeniable Roof.

No jagged, angry ridges here; just smooth, massive inclines,
Reflecting a mountain that already has a
Preeminent place, and so poses its challenge
By requiring an enormous effort of sheer *repetitive motion* activity.

Not to tempt the fates, though, we accorded Mount Elbert
The respect due her thin air and prolonged ledges.

So we commenced at midnight to pack our gear,
Then started the ascent at 2 A.M., and climbed for
Nearly 10 hours straight, summitting at 11:55 A.M.

No moments of insightful transcendence,
Only the sensation of burning thighs, and
The deep gulping gasp for air, more air —
Once we topped 13,000 feet or thereabouts.

Reflecting our deliberate caution, the descent
Took only a few hours less the ascent:
We were down by 7:30 P. M.

So what had we proved?

That not every task is infused with awe and wonder,

But that each communal experience adds

To our collective memory.

Insight and Situational Awareness

16. Doom

When I despair of reaching insight that will enlighten me,
My thoughts turn back to you, you hulking bulk of earth
Guiding my steps toward my unknowable lot in this life:
For however disguised my portion may be, it rests within
Your pathways guiding my course as I wander with the
Providential assurance of a sleepwalker, finding my direction
By placing my goal entirely subject to your roots ineluctably
Driving me toward my arcane destiny locked securely within
Your preordained fate for my body and soul.

Nothing I can do can avert my terminal rendezvous with my own
Occult kismet shaped as it is by a host of inscrutable factors over
Which I have no sway – rather they steer me toward your ultimate
Acme awaiting my advent at your pinnacle of perfection that had
Always eluded my grasp in the impermeable opaque mire below.

17. Toward Insight

I.

O mountain, how can it ever be
That we share an interdependent
Destiny?

You: stark and isolated, rest alone
In your majestic throne — your very own

"Fortress of Solitude" to which only the
Likes of our Superman can repair;

While I am far, far more than merely
"Alone" inside my rotting shell; for

Locked inside only me roils an
Existentialist "angst" that

I do realize, and dread: that I can
Be so much more that merely alone,
But can also be *lonely*:

A coward's pain that you can never know
Or feel — but do assuage mine just by
Being "there" for me.

II.

O mountain, no doubt you are there,
Brazenly occupying a territory
In the open air, without any sense
That you are

Surely a dumb character, but one
Who constantly hears the unfettered
Effluence of my fears, doubts, and grief;

A mute character who passively hears
But cannot actively listen, and
Whose very stolidity reassures me of my

Unique power to travel onward — eyes wide open —
To meet my all-too-human self-fashioned fate:

For only I have the potential to engage in the
Highest form of internal Socratic dialogue, which is
To *"know myself"*: for *"the unexamined life is not worth living"*.

By contrast, you can never "know thyself";
Indeed you are just "there".
Nor can you ever grasp the mesmerizing
Effect that you nonetheless project on all
Who fall under your natural sway.

Alan V. Goldman

III.

O mountain, no doubt you are there,
Brazenly occupying a territory in the open air,
Without any sense of encroaching on the space
That we all must try to share;

By what right do you assert your peremptory
Claim to our joint place under the Sun?
Or are you so oblivious of us humans that
We don't count in your calculus of right and wrong,
Such that

You self-justify your presence blocking my share
Of space and air by implicitly asserting that
"Might makes right" simply by your being "there"...

Hence you pose an eternal challenge to
All us climbers to subdue your insolent
Arrogance, by climbing your haughty faces and ridges,
And so lay low your perpetual challenge by rendering
You no more than a pitiful, fallen giant.

IV.

So I found myself in this harsh arena where the Sun's
Rays had just begun to filter into the sky as you lay unsuspecting
In your snug niche in the earth's crust — daring all to subdue
Your imposing bulk;

And I slowly roused myself from dreamland and reluctantly prepared
To re-enter the waking world:
O, it was so fraught with the petty realities of everyday life
As compared with the crystal clear, yet confused and unrealized
Grand notions locked away inside my mind —

But it feels all-too-easy to slip back and sleep on and on;
The snow ironically becoming an insulating layer — for a while —
Making me feel cozy and warm, lulling me to accept a dull insentience

Such that I find myself nearly paralyzed in my sleeping bag,
Loathe to unzip it and expose myself to the harsh elements
Before I had had a fair chance to don my appropriate attire
And fully "suit up" with my necessary gear, from crampons to
Helmet liner and all —

Armed with only my mountain axe
With which to examine your hidden places, and belay me in
A fall from your ever-daunting precipitous slopes.

Alan V. Goldman

18. My Self-Struggle

Sublime mountain vision enticing me on to exceed my ceiling
Of endeavor, ever-beckoning yet never satisfying my
Yearning to attain your spectre of perfection, itself not
Actually substantial but more like an apparition of my
Own confection, my own shadow, my apprehension of a
Realized ideal.

To penetrate the barrier between this world and your mountainous realm
Leaves me feeling as though I had overstepped some ban
That was designed since primordial times to serve as a taboo

Preventing humanity from gaining knowledge, not just of right and wrong,
But self-knowledge of the entire human condition.

And so I persist in pursuing your projected image of that realized ideal in
Order to obtain the promise of self-enlightenment that it holds forth as
Though a garland dangled before an ardent competitor — yet
Ever-eluding him.

19. *Moment of Clarity*

When my inner voice cries out to me,
I ask myself whether I am indulging in
The luxury of engaging in a private dialogue
Or whether some genuine insight has befallen me.

I banish all morose self-pity and instead focus on
The nature and quality of the language rattling about
My troubled mind and seek to filter out the extraneous
Noise from the almost palpable sensation of experiencing
The touch of the transcendent reality that governs all my
Perceptions of something Other, something beyond my own reality,

Of my own perception of the Divine. Life in the profane world has
Dulled my senses to perception of any reality outside my own being,
My own environment, my own needs and desires, as though I were
The very pinnacle of creation, and the world was constrained to
Revolve around me.

Only my resort to existentialist principles, which posit that I am nothing
But what I make of myself, that I can experience nothing outside the realm
Of my own perception and senses, and that, indeed, nothing else exists for
Me, brings me back to contemplation of that outside, inner communication
That intrusively made itself known to me:
The mountain existed; indeed, as was said, it was "*there*".

Then, and only then, do I recognize that there is an existence,
A world, a universe beyond my ken, which troubles me, for I do
Not control its spinning, nor govern its needs and wants as I can
Strive to do within my private, personal universe.

What of it? O, to know there is a reality outside my circumscribed
World is to be in touch with the universal truth, often obscured below,
But sometimes revealed at your airy summit where you speak to me of
Your abiding presence:

That you *are* "there".

And your ethereal multi-colored display at the transient
Moment of twilight evinced by Crepuscular Rays bursting
Through broken clouds refracting the Sun's golden light
Into all the variegated hues of the rainbow, from red through
Violet, inspires me to reflect upon my own internally mottled
Moods and sense of fleeting evanescence.

20. Eye of the Beholder

A shuddering rumble, a crackle, and then you settle down,
Serenely assured in your dominant place of uncontested
Preeminence in a sea of jumbled, jagged peaks;

Even your avalanches conform to the precept of your
Manifest command over the natural environment,
All without any intervention by mankind.

But don't you *need* mankind to behold and admire
Your holistic grandeur; or are you like the tree falling in an
Empty forest that makes no sound, for it might just
As well have fallen in a vacuum?

With no one to witness your sublime features,
How can you be "awe-inspiring" —
With no one present to be awed or inspired?

Would the *Mona Lisa* still retain her famously "enigmatic" smile
With no one there to be affected by it?
Indeed, how could her smile even be termed "enigmatic," or anything else,
Without the presence of a human observer to judge and react to it?

Like a work of art, then, is not a mountain's "beauty" likewise subjective?

For is not its wonder, too, perceived in the eye of a beholder?
Without a human observer, there would likewise be no "beauty" to behold
—

Just the existence of a shape of uninspiring rock.

In this sense, there exists a symbiotic, or interactive, relationship
Between mountains and humanity; and between a
Sea of peaks, and the beauty of the pageantry they
Project onto the eye of their beholder.

21. Rapture Unveiled

You provoke my ardor without stint, such that it relentlessly festers,
And abides with a maddening tenacity that ensnares all my thoughts with
A vain longing for any hint of your regard for my rapt enthrallment with
The prospect of your company — which presently seems ever more
Remote as the days wear on and on, with not a sign of recognition from
You, not even a glimmer of that special spark of acknowledgment
Signaling awareness.

What must I do to arouse at least your amenability?
May I ever entertain the notion of your potential accessibility? Is there no
Cunning stratagem that I may employ without its being perceived as
Nothing but a crafty artifice or wily device, blatantly transparent to anyone
Not already blinded by desire?

No: an honest passion eschews any course of action that even smacks of
Subterfuge.
I must *risk* all, exposing my secret, or gain nothing by resort to sleight of
Hand or feint of mind;

And the consequences can well be borne with the dignity that intrinsically
Accompanies integrity.

So my pursuit of your apex must remain nobly pristine, unbesmirched by
Any tawdry craving for my vision of your ever-disinterested, uncaring,
And remote zenith.

Force of the Mountain's Presence

22. Striving for the Top

Alluring like a majestic throne,
Its imposing summit always tauntingly
Visible while climbing beneath
Its maze of pathways below,
I wondered at its singular situation —
Passively awaiting its conquerors,
While silently watching them evade
Or overcome its defenses: its castle-like
Moats or *bergschrunds*;
Its trap doors or hidden crevasses:
Its crenellations or jagged rock walls,
Which seem so like ramparts or battlements
Challenging only those who would dare,
To win, as the motto goes.

Win what? The satisfaction of sitting
In the throne — a symbol of both physical
Mastery and of psychological dominion.

23. Wild Structure

A boom, a crack — whoosh,
The echo of rolling thunder
Resonating inside my body —
All these are harbingers

Of the trembling, crushing
Naked power of the powdery
White death that flattens all before it
Without discrimination,

And then transforms into
A sliding slurry that
Engulfs and swallows all

Hapless objects in its path
Before congealing into a
Cement-like substance

Indiscriminately poured
Into an amorphous mold.

So, too, flow my uncorralled thoughts
Around, above, below, and through
The twisted paths inside my mind,

Into the liminal horizons
Lurking in-between the
Thoughts that careen about
The ill-defined boundaries
Barely structuring my ideas,

One from another, 'till
They merge into an amalgam
That has an internal coherence,
Like the residue of an avalanche,
Existing for good or ill —

Its very being, however ill-formed,
Serving as its own rationale.

Alan V. Goldman

24. *Renewal*

Each time I review your
Massive mountain wall anew
Rejuvenation does ensue
While my spirit can pursue
All that is within my purview.

And what does my demesne encompass?
Is it all that I can possess?
Or only that which I can bless
By my having duly venerated it
Through subjecting myself to its fickle whims,

Thereby renewing my right to occupy its
Throne without having desecrated it.

Likewise, I have thus not denigrated
My own sphere of action that
I have so carefully aggregated

By not having deviously manipulated
My unalienable right to explore
My own view of happiness.

And *this* is the essence
Of the spirit of effervescence
That animates the climber's quest
For the trial that will
Manifest the path for all Seekers
After *The Freedom of the Hills*.

25. The Winds Speak

Swirling about the silent slabs,
The mountain winds speak with
The ineffable wisdom borne of
Hearing the cries and confessions
Of all the lost and forgotten who
Regret having chosen a desultory path:

A way studded by fortuitous rewards gained through
Haphazard actions, not earned through merit,
But littered by random circumstance and serendipity.

O, how they yearn to have chosen the way
Of pursuing success by risking failure and
Exposing themselves to peril in search of
Self-knowledge about their limits of frightful
Human endurance.

For in these climbers' defeats are untold glories
That far surpass any ignoble victories claimed by
Those who think they have found a plan to cheat fate:
And the winds continue to twirl about and about.

26. Paean to Being

Slicing through the open sky
Your features give form to
Where there had been only
A devoid expanse without
Character or direction:

Vacant space no more,
Now imbued with design,
Further magnified by suffusion
With the purposeful intent imparted
By the skeletal features
Now occupying your empty space
And by the climber's many storied travails.

O, if only those features could speak,
They would tell of the desperate chances
Ventured on their extended flanks
Imparting human meaning to their otherwise silent stone,
And your once vacant space.

So the rocky framework of the mountain's presence
Has rescued us from the
Empty environs by furnishing the *mise-en-scene*
For climbers to act out their human dramas
In the blank sky, no longer a desolate void of
Airy nothingness, but the backdrop for an active
Part of nature's being.

27. Day-Dream

Just when I despaired of ever attaining my goal,
I dared to day-dream and reconceive of the unique image
That had propelled me to where I now was,
Summoning the spirit of the unbounded mountain vista
That was unfolding before me as I ascended ever higher:

Its scooped-shaped amphitheater;
Its narrowly fluted wall-grooves that funneled spin-drift together with
The driving wind; my own hesitant steps secured here by hollow ice
Screws linked to carabiners threaded with my 9 mm water-resistant,
Kernmantle rope attached to my full body harness (chest and seat),
Double-looped back (*i.e.*, "pull-through proof") into my harness loop,
Attached using the iconic figure-eight rope formation holding me fast to
The well-secured rope, so that any fall would be arrested far short of
Suffering failure (*unless all* the ice screws ripped out as I gained
Momentum).

I was endeavoring to limit the factor of random chance that can never be
Wholly squeezed out of the climbing equation — only hemmed-in and
Tempered by prudent foresight, born of experience: *that's* why we use
Seemingly mind-numbing checklists of deeds done or to do so that as little
As possible may be left to memory, which can fail, or worse yet, play
Cruel tricks on our minds.

Reinvigorated by the recollection of my studious preparations, I pushed
Upward and toward an unknown outcome but hopeful of achieving unity
With your symbol of perfection, the ultimate expression of your projection
Of power, your summit region's highest peak.

212

Likewise, down below, I meticulously strived to create a safety net of Excuses in the event that all my carefully crafted plans and determined Efforts at becoming one with you still came to naught – lest my quest be Seen as having been misconceived from its inception, predestined to an Ignoble doom.

28. *The Prosaic and the Pristine*

When I turn for solace toward your form,
When I seek peace of mind in your thoughts
Is when I reach for the well-spring of knowledge
That ultimately governs the motive for all our choices,
Relying on "no one but myself" and my perception
Of being guided by some source of wisdom,
Be it manifest for all to see, or as recondite and
Esoteric that it hides even from me:

Hidden from scrutiny by the idly curious so
That it eludes prosaic inspection and dwells among
The abstract concepts that we all know somehow shape
Our fate — and so abstruse as to block the vision of the
Uninformed masses, who would peer into the recesses
Of your churning process that molds the outcome of
Our daily predicaments;

Hidden from the prying eyes of the high-born who
Would seek advantage through foreknowledge of
Things yet to come;

Hidden from the evil and innocent alike who must
Grapple with their destinies like boxers locked in a clinch;

Hidden notions from themselves lest they contaminate
The purity of their essential qualities that make bare
Ideas come alive and relate to the mundane world.

29. Perpetual Challenge

What is a mountain but an abstraction reduced to a thing for us to
Surmount? Indeed, humanity grows, even thrives, only by having some
Formidable obstacle to conquer, a challenge fairly to meet.
Absent such an impediment obstructing our way to achievement of some
Worthy Goal, our spirit withers from pure stagnation and inanition.

So let not anyone mischaracterize a mountain as no more than an idle form
Having no function but to be to be circumvented in our life's journey;
No, its very being is at the center of our nature to wrestle with the scruples
Of our own self-doubt about the intrinsic value of how we meet all our
Struggles to overcome the varied blockages we encounter in life that
Would impair our exercise of liberty; here, the innate "Freedom of the
Hills" to wander where we would in the uninhibited exercise of our own
Discretion.

The mountain thus beckons us to top its summit simply because it is,
Indeed, "there". To have evaded its eternal challenge, its come-hither call,
Is to have evaded the full demurrer of that challenge: the mountain asks
"So what about *my* summit" — and we are constrained to reply that we will
Someday trample it, all in due course, at a time and manner of our
Choosing.

30. Despondency Challenged

I sing a song of morose desolation
That bemoans my anguish, sorrow, and
Long-forlorn grief, while I languish without
Relief from my rueful lament, tinged with
Regret that my sacrifices taint my triumphs, mar my
Achievements, and sap my hard-won glories
Of their latent consoling powers:

My grief always prevails in a putrescent sink of
"what ifs"— for it festers as if in a stopped-up
Cesspool, never draining its overbearing melancholia
So as to fill all my emotions with a perpetual remorse,
Leaving me to marinate in a stew of self-reproach —

Except when I think once more on the sharp aspect of your
Brazenly insolent Northwest face, which smirks at my shortcomings,
And would blithely ridicule all my virulent tribulations,
Time after time, and then again;

Thus irking, arousing, and then
Summoning me to marshal all my being *to try my fate once more*,
so as to silence forever your infuriatingly mute challenge:

Eternal hope thus dispels the dreary gloom cast by your silent shadow —

Hope that blinds one and all so as to mask the true dimensions of
Your treacherous slopes;

Hope that is said to spring eternal, like the hope born of youth;

Hope that I can meet self-expectations on your forbidding flanks
While knowing that these hopeful expectations can all be dashed by one
wave of clinical despair that would erode my resolve to test the limits of
your pity.

O, take pity on me, and give me this one last chance to contribute
Something of value to the life of *my* mind, and, more importantly,
To enable me to touch the inner life of others.

*Evaluating the Moments
of a Mountain's Reality*

31. *Reality Imprisoned*

What is it that drives one to reach for the nameless moment
That captures our perception of time and motion in the
Vacuum of a personal space, where our actions are arrested,
Forever held still in perpetuity, and stripped naked for all to behold
Their inner nature, devoid of any pretense and laid bare for all
To dissect their essential qualities without regard for their
Intrinsic privacy?

Why reach for that ineffable picture of perfection, frozen
In unnatural eternity, where the truth of the moment
Has no past and no future, but glows with a grim intensity
As though ripped out of the present, its wound still shimmering
At the edges where it was detached from the normal flow
Of time?

Because the reality of any moment, even the most dear, can be
Captured and held in a prison by resort to one's infinite
Imagination, a faculty which admits of no limitation, and cannot
Be corralled by mundane parameters of the place before or after,
But thrives in the exercise of its potential to extend the present,
And would wither and shrivel but for its assertion over mere matter
Caught in the web of progressive time and ever-expanding space.

Thus each moment of reality can be experienced to its fullest
In the here and now and be forever so enshrined — its picture
Infused with boundless meaning — though it be infinitely encompassed
In a singular point in time, *e.g.,* in our imminent attainment of the summit.

32. *The Consummate Barrier:*
A Journey of Outer and Inner Exploration

Between here and there lies the undiscovered region
Intrinsic to a void of non-being, of an expanse of apparent nothingness
That perplexes the climber's body and mind with the desolation
That lures the will to pursue its fate and play out its string 'till the
End of time, or of whatever will confront it on the other side
Of this side of eternity.

Such a desolate region creates a magnet of ineludible attraction
Towards the unknown that entices one's curiosity, and o'er sways
One's better judgment that cries out: *Halt!* – for that way lies forbidden
Insight into the nature and quality of one's own. internally-driven
Desires to explore the regions of one's own mind, under the pretense
Of exploring the external landscape of the unknown terrain meretriciously
Seeming to lie just ahead, but in fact reposing deep within the unexplored
Layers of encrusted grime concealing our nature from ourselves:
Thus our own ambiguity does sometimes restrain us.

For what the climber may discover about himself on his journey of
Exploration may far surpass what he uncovers about himself and his
Outward *desiderata*: the nub is that every climber secretly harbors
Some dread that he will discover more about himself, such as his
Fears and limits, during the course of his journey than he will about
The nominal object of his physical search across the boundaries lying
Beyond the known barrier of his physical world.

So that which forever haunts the climber is what may be revealed to
Others, and to himself, about his own nature during his quest, far more
Than what he may ever discover about the features of the terrain blocking
His way.

This simultaneous dichotomy between the outer and inner realities that
May be discovered by the climber's journey confounds the drive to attain
Completion of every climber's goal, the summit, and like an anchor
Dragging along the sea bottom's floor, secretly encumbers the drive to
Achieve knowledge of new environs for fear of what they may inwardly
Expose about him in the course of their outward discovery.

33. On the Nature of Perceived Reality

If I could pause time on the surmounting of a summit,
Then you would know of the exuberant transcendence
That overtakes me in that special moment of detached,
Timeless ecstasy – known to some climbers as the
Rapture of the Heights, or *Hypoxic Euphoria,* as the Doctors
Call it – a state of mind wherein the brain, partially
Starved of oxygen, and elated at having achieved success,
Acts such that one's conduct resembles nitrogen narcosis –
The feared "*Rapture of the Deep,*" yet displays a peculiar
Inebriation without any dulling of the senses; indeed, just the
Opposite obtains: an *intensification* of the senses prevails,
Transforming the climber into a seeker after a reality otherwise
Closed to mere mortals going about their day-to-day routine, a
Pattern of monotonous existence that the climber is driven to escape.

It is this heightened state of awareness that is the *desiderata* treasured
By all who climb with the purpose of bursting the bonds of normality that
Ordinarily confine all to a given role in existence – a moment of insight
That we Seekers wish could be prolonged indefinitely at the summit, but
Which inevitably evaporates in an evanescent moment of time that can be
Forever recalled but never prolonged:

Thus fades worldly glory that can appear just as fast as it hastens to flee.

34. The Power of Attraction

Like a monstrous ogre, you would seem to reject all suitors who brazenly
Dare to scale your slopes without displaying due deference to your
Imposing shape;

Yet climbers still flock to your faces, ridges, snow fields, and narrow
Couloirs without invitation, knowing full well the penalty for failure may,
At the least, be the indefinite termination of their relationship with you.

Maybe in another ten years?

By then your silent power of attraction may have even faded a bit so that I
Can prosecute the lay of my campaign without being overwhelmed
By the grip of your majesty; unfortunately, though, a mountain's time is
Reckoned on a different scale than that of a human being's.

True, your gravitational-like pull on all who fall within the path of your
Orbit dissipates as one draws further and further away from the form of
Your mass.

Yet when one is subject to your full puissance, your draw is like that of a
Nubile woman whose beckoning scent potently wafts through the air
Around her inviting shape, and it is *then* that you exert your special
"Come-hither" quality of attraction that lures every climber to test his
Mettle against your tempting form.

In this manner, your power of attraction mentally outlasts even the decay
Of age, so that everyone can entertain thoughts of struggle and conquest
No matter the situation at hand.

35. The Love of the Things in this World
And the Spiritual Quest for the Summit
Honoring the Brotherhood of the Rope

When I ponder over whether my life was squandered in search of your
Perfection, I turn to contemplation of the "value" of your presence in this
World, and meditate on how life would have been had I not pursued the
Impalpable, the inchoate, the intangible at the expense of seeking solely
Worldly goods;

In this regard, I never cease to be astonished at how it is that your dirt,
Your ground, your routes, and summit are the very quintessence of the
Most mundane, the most palpable physicality of this life, and,
Concomitantly, can represent the most aspirational notions of an ethereal
Vision of a *purity of motive* in "climbing for its own sake" and a *nobility
Of faith* in one's rope partner that are too good for this world.

If your bulk can encompass both the most material realities and the highest
Spiritual impulses, you leave me perplexed and astounded; after all, who
Am I to judge your import in this world or the next, much less whether
You substantially constitute something of value?

36. *Last Thoughts on a Forlorn Conclusion and a New Beginning*

Can mountain memories be revisited without fear of falling into an
Analytical, lugubrious reverie?
Must our recollections be overlaid by the burden of second-sight?
When can we permit ourselves to abandon the remembrance of past events
And former friends? Will our selfish conduct in letting go thereafter haunt
Our enjoyment of life? How can our senses ever be washed clean?

I'll tell you when: when the burden of guilt for the memory of those left
Behind is purged from our minds; and this can never occur until we
Liberate ourselves from all the altruistic impulses that had motivated us in
The flush of our youth. Until then, we must wallow in the mire of things
Gone by, and of thoughts fearfully misprisioned by the clutches of regret;
And we must reckon with the harsh bill that must be paid for our peace of
Mind, abandoning insouciant dwelling in the innocence of times past.
Until then, we will forever dwell in the darkness of the endless night of
Oblivion that floods our senses and engulfs our minds – and its perpetually
Whispering in our ears: *"lest we forget"*…

37. *My Finale*

Mountain, mountain, are you there,
Or inside me, and consuming an unfair
Share of authentic infinity ?

Either way, you engulf my being
To the point where I can hardly tell
Where my thoughts leave off, and
Your reality creeps in.

Thus, I pause to reflect upon the impact
That you have had on me, and that which
I have had on my image of you, and ponder:

Is our relationship symbiotic or parasitic, for
I wonder whether I have imbued you with too
Much of my hopes, and animated you with too
Many of my dreams and with the life of my mind,

Such that you have become the
Oracle of my personal destiny, and I but the refrain?

My whole being revolts at the notion that your
Influence has controlled my thoughts in a
Deterministic way, and by contrast celebrates
The concept that the exercise of my free will
Through my choices made along the way shaped
The outcome of my life's little play.

Afterthoughts

38.   In Search of One's Private Peace of Mind

As I viewed your imposing bulk, my stomach began to shiver;
As I scanned your stark features, I accepted your challenge, however bitter;
For I resolved that your craggy appearance was not going to make me a quitter;
Au contraire, for I could conceive of no end that could possibly be fitter.

Even more, I realized that I would not respect you if you were just a snow dome;
Nor could I respect my endeavor to surmount you as anything but a sign of
some banal, empty syndrome
If you proved an unworthy antagonist, fit for nothing but residing in your home,
Overlooked by Seekers for some transformative moment of wisdom.

Thus, I persevere in penetrating your narrow, sharp series of spires,
Because I feel they might reveal something hidden about the world, or me
While I hang precariously on my complex web of wires;
Trusting implicitly that you are incapable of guile but exude enlightenment
That only inspires me to plunge ever onward in search of my own,
fictive *Dulcinea* who forever strums alluringly on her lyre.

39. The Next Breath

We planned in anticipation of great feats to be done
Just as if tomorrow can be expected always to come.
We seemed to see so far down the route to be won
Though when viewed, *a la longue,* our doings could never
Rest assured they would be deemed worthy, or even practicable,
According to some.

Nonetheless, we pressed onward with the certainty of the beguiled,
Believing in ourselves that nothing could mislead or upset our well-devised
Strategy for the conquest of our goal, but without accounting for the
Random element inherent in the nature of things that could generate a problem

Rooted in the fundamental mutability and fluctuating fortune of actual contact
With the natural world in all its fickle moods and unknown
Features -- such that time itself became so compressed that there
Was scarcely any *opportunity* to contemplate "the future" much
Beyond the scope of our very next step, nor time to make plans for
The future beyond taking just the next breath.

40. Reflections on My Creative Process

The very intensity of my feelings forms
An inescapable part of my creative process,
Which itself drives the volatility of my moods.

Indeed, in that special moment when I feel
The potency of the universe welling up inside me,
Though still contained at my extremities, then I
Know that I possess an infinite potential to let loose
The essential energy of life itself.

And yet I am tossed about by a mortal storm that
Floods my emotions and, after its winds abate,
Leaves my sails to luff, uselessly flapping to and fro,
Caught in the spiritual doldrums.

Some time thereafter, my creative processes do slowly
Gather once again, permitting me to resume engaging in
That most human endeavor of indulging in the ability
To love and to hate -- the most emotive of expressions
Unique to the human species in both their nature and quality.

41. Silent Sentinel

And there it stood... a monolith of
Cracked and jagged ledges,
Weather-beaten over eons of time --
But brazenly defiant in all its full glory
Of the naked display of its raw power
That co-exists with what one
Perceptive Amazon reader (Primer, Nov. 16, 2022)
Has described as the *"brutal beauty"*
Atop a summit's peak --

Where it still stands watch over the curving horizon --
Lest we see too far.

Our little band of intrepid Seekers
Nonetheless dared to challenge this
Crumbling giant's mass unroped,
For its rotten sedimentary bulk cannot
Support the weight that high tension
Protection would impose, and the
Frigid but not turbulent weather was O
So perfectly inviting.

And so we persevered in our ascent even
After the weather conditions had deteriorated
Far past the point where we would never have
Initiated the climb. But, caught in the trap of,
Not intentional *hubris*, but instead that of

"Plan-Continuation-Bias" -- a sinister syndrome
Against which every mountaineer must guard --
We were drawn ineluctably upwards in an attempt to achieve
Completion, *now that we were ever so close* to our
Mind and body's goal;

Thus, we were beckoned onward by an insidious desire
That we just *had* to continue, having already invested so
Much energy and expectations, such that we could not
Reconcile ourselves to abandoning the challenge posed
By the dominant mass confronting us.

Finally, we ignominiously retreated, and not as a roped
Group, but one-by-one, from where none belonged any
Longer.

But, as human beings, we will always need *some* daunting
Challenge, or else we would stagnate and
Shrivel away.

Alan V. Goldman

42. Fate Plays a Hand

As we again approached the solitary spire of slick blue ice,
I knew that this endeavor was akin to rolling loaded dice
Where we could become prisoners of our own device,
Trapped by our own commitment to paying the price --
Caught in the unyielding grip of the malignant
Syndrome of Plan-Continuation-Bias, where one continues
Impulsively onward, even when conditions arise -- just before
Attaining the summit -- that, had they existed *at the outset* of
The attempt, one would have declined to commence at all.

No matter having failed before and having lost all twice --
For success on this spire had become an all-consuming vice
That warped our judgment in its pursuit, despite any sacrifice
In search of a vainglorious prize that reflected but a slice
Of nature, where there's *no* sense of "entitlement" under any guise of "justice":

We felt already so committed to our quest for the vindication of our effort
To perceive that a mind-warping poison had blinded us to the fact that
We were enmeshed in the menace of a Bias that had taken hold
Of our struggle, for having already sacrificed *so much* to reach
Thus far that it felt like a craven act of *self-betrayal **not*** to continue only
Three pitches further, and bask in our "just" rewards, ignoring the ever-
Morphing conditions on the mountain that had always defined our destiny.

So, the climber must always retain his sense of
His limitations, and be ready to accept the gentle down-slope, or be
crushed by his

Self-manufactured sense of entitlement not to turn back – irrespective of What the conditions mandate.

43. *Mountain Justice*

Nothing shakes my world so much as watching tyros fumble in bad form on
Your most recondite slopes, for to go "where no man has gone before"
Is in itself no justification for being where one ought not to be just for
The sake of setting foot on untrodden ground in a desperate
Quest to fill in a "blank on the map" with the imprint of their clumsy steps,
Vainly seeking to create meaning where there had been none before.

That is not sound adventure, nor existential statement, but rather foolhardy,
Wanton desecration of your innate privacy without deference to the
Reverential method that respects your pristine ground, but instead uses the
Mountain to further one's *own* naked ambition without first having paid the
Requisite dues in training, experience, and learning what it's like to survive
Your inescapable, savage reprisal in the form of broken bones and spirit.

For I had seen someone fall to his ineradicable fate, not just
Cut the rope blindly without knowing whether such action would prove
To be the ultimate act of finality.

44. Time Warp in the High Country?

Around and around we whirl, concerned with this day, the next day, or the
day before and after that,
As the mountain stands fast -- oblivious of the passage of time;

Are *we* "time's fool," (for *love* is *not*, as the Bard has told us in *Sonnet 116*),
While we ourselves prance to and fro, ordinarily with
Little respect for any one moment in itself...

But "A thing of beauty is a joy forever," as Keats contends (in *Endymion*)
Dwindling not with time's passage; certainly, the *idea* of
Beauty is perpetual and cannot be parceled up into mere fragments of time.

As *climbers* know, however, an entire lifetime can indeed be reduced to
Only "*the next step taken now*" (see my poem, **The Power of Now**, p.16),
Or can be felt as wholly extant, *i.e.*, "frozen" in one motion at a time;

Moreover, the infinity of time itself can seem captured in but fractions of a
Second when measuring one's "reaction-time" to this or that exigency;
Indeed, time itself can be felt to have *stopped* when one is
Caught up in moments of tense *anticipation of impending things* about to come.

The climber, however, knows not to fret over the happenings of one day or
another;

For as the saying now going around goes:
What is today if not yesterday's tomorrow?

The climber's days likewise meld into each other, while all other profane
Things are put on hold when pursuing a *transcendent* goal: *i.e.*, attaining
The eternal Summit.

45.   A Musing on the Human Condition

Is not the world's pervasive suffering, its *Weltschmerz*, sufficient reason to
abandon all hope for the future?
Are we not so besotted with the world's misery, its *lacrimae rerurm,* such
that there can never be any respite?
Won't any hope for the future founder on the lugubrious woe that inhabits
Everything around us, and also penetrates into our human spirit, our very
own being, polluting even
Our God-breathed spirit, our inner *neshuma?*

I maintain that it is only if we **choose** to pursue one inherent human
inclination -- that leading to eternal darkness --
Over the other inherent human inclination leading to perpetual light, can the
forces of despair triumph forever.

For only humanity has the power to know good from evil; and only
Humanity can perceive the vast forces of darkness
Arrayed against the world;

Most critically, Humanity has the power of free will to choose what course
of action it will pursue in the struggle to set
The flawed world aright.

Therein lies the hope of the prophets:
To *awaken* the good inclination over the evil, and
Point the way toward redemption of the world's sorrows, achieving a kind of
Salvation for the generations to come.

46. *Enduring Love*

Why do you arouse me with nothing more than the crossing of your legs?
Why do you provoke me with nothing more than the *sotte voce* purr of
your throat?
Why do you spur me to a feverish pitch with nothing more than the sway
of your hips to and fro?
How can I fail to alert you to my impulsive urge to reach for your
stimulating figure?
And how can I suppress my urgent attraction to your form without alerting
your attention to my ceaseless longing,
As I furtively struggle to conceal my would-be innocent, but deceitful
glance at the ground -- without being caught
In the very act of doing so?

Only by cultivating some genuine familiarity on the basis of shared interests
That might deactivate your finely-tuned radar, which otherwise would
unmask the course of my campaign
Driven by my over-heated vision of your pulsating sway.

It's sometimes said that relationships founded on a shared intense
experience,
E.g., of a mutual danger (like an accident on a mountain) don't survive the
"test of time," but shrivel as the shock of
The shared trauma, without more, inevitably recedes into oblivion.

If that's so, then how much less can a relationship founded merely on some shared

Abstract or vicarious experience of imagined intensity survive, where one based on an actual,

Disastrous life-event inevitably retreats into the recesses of memory?

So a lasting relationship must be based not only on superficial attraction, for as we

All have heard, "beauty fades," but also on some shared sense of enduring values

That will *outlast* the heat of passion.

Alan V. Goldman

47.   Is the Game Worth the Candle?

Are the rewards of "mountaineering" worth the effort required to attain its goal?

All this evaluation occurs in a subjective state of mind about a subjective perception of both what that "effort" is,
And what that "reward" is, considered as a whole.

Therefore, one must first *define* the endeavor of "mountaineering" *itself*,
for the complete "mountaineering experience"
Consists of not only planting one's feet upon a summit, but also encompasses
what came *before* and *after* the climb is
clumb, including:

all the *preparation, planning*, and *packing* that occurred *before* the climax
of the climb, part of which can determine the course of events yet to come;

as well as the *telling and retelling* of one another's experiences that transpired
during the climb -- all of which are recounted *after* the climb is done.

Thus, "mountaineering" is a unitary *Gestalt* that is *more*
Than the sum of its parts, and the "reward" must include the
Entirety of the whole in making any judgment weighing the amount of
"effort" required to attain this as its "goal," namely:

the experiential participation in the group *mythos* of the mountain's folklore.

Now, how to assess the "effort" required to attain this expansive reward?

Or, what effort will a man expend in exchange for this award?

Certainly all his so-called "best efforts," even at the expense of supreme
suffering and sorrow -- but

Not the willful sacrifice of even one man's tomorrow,
For then the climber would have surely lost his way on the
Way to the top:

  the celebration of the group would necessarily be irredeemably
diminished by an infinite amount --
even by the loss of a single human life, the worth of which cannot be
"weighed" (except against the loss of more lives than one):

  because a life cannot be replaced by, nor equated with, the sum of any
material deeds (however nobly they may be won) --

  a single life being woven into the fabric of the entire universe; indeed,
each life is its own microcosm, the life-of-its-mind being unique, and thus
is not ours to give and take in trade for some material gain (however much
it may prove to be fun);

  for the loss of one life is not compensable, it is irreparable.

So one must always bear in mind:
The mountain will always be there (in the human scale of time),
And, *if* you are present, can be attempted in another climb,

For we are no more than a passing vapor.

48. *Perpetual Motion*

It should strike quickly, definitively, and irrevocably -- not linger like
The long wining of Autumn winds which intermittently wax and wane,
Arousing false hope that Winter will not descend upon us ineluctably.

What good is served by prolonging one's *exeunt* stage left when there
Is no point to playing out our string, to paying out our rope in piecemeal,
Grudging fits and starts of alternating "slack" and "tension," 'till reaching the
End at the line's blocking knot, then acting as if we were surprised at its
All-too-familiar advent that requires no perspicacity to forecast its finality?

None I dare say; yet sometimes we are resentful, willful, and obstinate,
Denying the reality that all things are in a state of transience, the sole
Universal constant, which will not be denied by even our most steadfast,
Intransigent mode of irksome conduct. Selfish beings are we, loathe to
Apprehend that the self itself will be submerged to make way for another,
And that we should embrace, not recoil from, the workings of Nature.

49.   On the Brink of A New Life?

Atop the summit of the peak I had just surmounted, its northeast escarpment seemed enveloped by the predawn, bluish-white glow of the Sun's emergent aurora, as my shadow itself seemed to shimmer, Back-lit by the diaphanous illumination during the transient moments of the not-quite-risen Sun;

It was *then* that I felt the palpable, penetrating presence of something Outside myself that animated my inner being with the blinding light of Sunrise --

And it was only then that I truly comprehended the meaning of the Ancient prophetic proclamation, as I confessed to myself:

"Holy, holy, holy is the Lord of Hosts; the whole earth is full of His Glory" (Isaiah 6:3).

So, was my willful exercise of self-choice, my existentialist, self-directed path, actually subordinate to some power greater than I could ever hope to be?

Yes, *but only if* I believed that God dwelt among us -- for without God, we are said to be desperately devoid of purpose, perpetually consumed with self-doubt, and compelled to forge our own way alone, forever asking ourselves the question:

"Is God dead?" Or, more exactly -- and disturbingly -- "Was He ever alive"?

And can we ever afford to abandon our perpetual self-questioning?

To this, we must firmly answer: "No," at the peril of abandoning the Quest for empirical, scientific truth in favor of a faith based on an a *priori* apprehension of the truth.-- for Scripture itself proclaims, in a well-known proverb, that:

"Great is the truth and it prevails!" or in the Latin Vulgate translation: *"Magna est veritas et praevalet!"*
(1 *Esdras* 4:41.)

50. *Falling Drops*

Falling drops of autumn rain,
You never make me strain
To perceive your occult domain;
It's enough for me to know
That you flow from *something hidden*
In the perpetual cycle of moisture driven
By the force of gravity -- God's own "1G"
To reach places that mortals are forbidden to be --
Who nonetheless insolently strain to reach for the sky.

51. Keeping up the Pace

Muffled footsteps crunch delicately in the freshly frozen snow;
I gingerly follow in the footsteps of my leader, stretching to plant
My feet in the tracks he's made ahead of me so as not to duplicate
Effort by breaking new trail; yet the length of my gait is not as lanky
As his so that I continually fall just short of his already sunken path,
Making my way a stressful struggle "to keep up" with the leader's pace by
treading in his footsteps,

Or else fall behind, out of synchronicity with his tempo, thereby testing
His patience in having frequently to hold back on account of me, thus
Arresting his natural rhythm and straining his patience at the tyro

Lagging behind him, and log-jamming the line of trekkers behind *him* --
all strung out affixed to the guide's lead rope, and disrupting their almost
haptic sense of intimacy with that communal bond as the rope randomly
develops either slack or tension,

Reducing their rhythm to an erratic staccato of stop-and-start movements,
trying their patience with my ungainly, lumbering, jerky steps leading to
nowhere, slowly.

52. Peculiar Progression Toward the Far Distant Unknown

I trudged, step after step, in a monotonous regimentation, then I made a so-called "dynamic" move -- a kind of *kinetic lunge* that propelled me into a spot that I couldn't have reached without having let go of all my carefully placed protection, thus yielding to the propulsive impetus of momentum to carry me toward my desired position.

In this insidious way, my climb proceeded unnaturally, in virtual slow-motion --
Punctuated by fits and starts, by slumps and booms, of unnaturally *ir*regular
Dynamic motion that added spice to my persistent, unwavering efforts that otherwise
Would have led me into a trance-like condition of inwardly listless inertia, so
That each time I took another step, I would have become all-the-more enwrapped in a languorous indolence that would cause a self-induced state of *mentally detached* progression -- locked inside a microcosm, and not driven by thoughts of getting from point "A" to point "B," as we naturally operate,

In such a condition, I would be led almost helplessly onward (not unlike a sleepwalker) to reach what had appeared, down below, as a *"hopelessly remote"* Point "B," *i.e.,* the Summit, and to an unknown fate beyond.

53. *Rumination upon Reaching the Summit*

When I attain the summit, just what have I obtained?
There's no "there" there -- just an airy space of nothingness;
And yet I've achieved everything I set out to do, have I not?
So what was the force that pursued me during my quest for the summit:
A realization of perfection, the reification of a dream, or
The concretion of an abstract set of ideas about my goal?

But none of these accomplishments is sufficient to explain the
Exhilaration of reaching the top of an inert mass that had somehow
Exerted a monomaniacal drive within me to surmount it -- and yet then
Failed to greet me with a tangible reward.

O, yes, at the summit of each of Colorado's 54 "Fourteeners"
(Peaks over 14,000') there *is* a quaint cylinder containing a "log sheet"
Where one can inscribe his or her name and date of ascension --
Like a lawyer signing a property deed -- a paradigm that's supposed to
impart some measure of tangible "success" in terms of possession --

But all that such a record can actually reflect is the completed fact of the
ascension; it can't substitute for the sensation of *owning the moment of
attaining the top*: O no, that's reserved for the secret recesses of memory,

And certainly, such a record cannot reflect the substance of the
circumstances we have left behind us *down below* -- all erased from our
minds during our singular pursuit of the Summit,

Likewise not communicable in such a fashion is that which each climber
has left behind him or herself *on the mountain* itself.

Such a residue forges an image of each climber's effort that becomes
imprinted on the tissue of the mountain's eternal lore.

54. Delicacy Amidst Terror

Lithely scampering across the miniscule ledges of a precipitous ravine,
I sensed a mood of refractory willfulness coming over me;
And none dare call it by its secretive name, for none was keen to face the
Gorge's treacherous allure when even I knew that I ought to let it be:

Yet the thrill of reckless danger while delicately evading the manifest
terror down below, seized my thoughts,

And beckoned me onward, momentarily causing a warm shiver of guilty
pleasure to course through the length of my spine (not unlike what Odysseus
felt when, though bound to the mast, he heard the song of the Sirens);

As I groped for the safety-line, only to find it entangled with age-old,
hoary knots,
I abruptly realized that my aberrant flippancy about an my precarious
environs,

Was a providential sign that I had finally burst free
From the invisible, imagined bubble of safety that had so often enveloped me;

I was prepared to plunge headlong through the ether, hurtling
To an uncertain fate, transcending good and ill, while basking
In the sheer ecstasy of indulging in the senseless and
Wanton activity of climbing, which was so fraught with overt
And hidden *repetitive hazards* that apparently tempted me to entertain the
Notion that I was possessed by a lurking *Todestrieb* (or hidden death-wish) --

Entirely beyond the comprehension of the gawking on-lookers below, who
could not know
that I had desired only to demonstrate my mastery over my environment,
arguably falling prey to delusions of grandeur:

For I have no rightful prerogative to determine what is
A worthy life or a just death.

252

55. *Expression of the Will*

As I acknowledged in a prior poem,
There's no "there" there, atop a peak;
Only the interlude it affords us to face
Reality, and to put into perspective our
Everyday troubles that we have left behind
Down below, which are soothed by a moment
Of serene isolation, of supreme contemplation
Of the meaning of our travails on our way to the top.

Such satisfaction is enough to satiate even *my* soul,
And to empower me to revel in my accomplishment
In achieving at least three *desiderata* that drew
Me to climbing in the first place:

To experience the state of mind known as positive "Flow";

To make a willful "*Existentialist statement*" of my purpose in just *being*; and,

To proclaim my "unalienable right" to enjoy my chosen form of the
"*Pursuit of Happiness*" by indulging in the unfettered *wanderlust*
that comprises the mountaineer's notion of "*The Freedom of the Hills*".

In this way, I express *my will* in three different modalities, be it:

(1) to concentrate so as to attain a state of intense focus ("*Flow*");
(2) to declare my freedom to be, just as I choose to be ("*Existentialist*"); and
(3) to rejoice at my unfettered "pursuit of happiness" -- roaming
wherever my will leads me ("*The Freedom of the Hills*").

Curtail any one of these three, and the perception of freedom is truncated,
indeed, corrosively undermined.

Beyond this, one can understand that a climber's "will" is an assertion of his
mastery over his *natural environment*, and of his mastery over *himself*.

---FIN---